CHRIST IN THE CHAOS

How the Gospel Changes Motherhood

Kimm Crandall
Cruciform Press | March, 2013

For Justin,
whose love and grace for me keep me going.
And for Grace, Jonah, Lily, and Jackson.
Without you my life would lack adventure. May you
grow up knowing you are loved and adored by the
greatest Super Hero of them all.

– Kimm Crandall

CruciformPress

"What an amazingly wild and wise, disruptive and delighting, freeing and focusing book on gospel parenting my new friend, Kimm Crandall, has written. The heck with this just being for mothers, Kimm's book is for every parent willing to take the stewardship of children and the riches of the gospel seriously. This is one of the most helpful and encouraging books on parenting I've read in the past twenty years, of any length. Kimm writes as a multi-child mom and a grace-saturated woman who understands the exhausting demands of good parenting and the inexhaustible supply of God's grace. This will be a book you will want to give to parents, to-be parents, and grandparents."

Scotty Smith, Founding Pastor of Christ Community Church, Franklin, TN. Author of *Objects of His Affection*, *Restoring Broken Things*, and *Everyday Prayers: 365 Days to a Gospel Centered Faith*

"Although Kimm Crandall's message in *Christ in the Chaos* would revive any soul longing for the breath of the gospel of grace, I am especially eager to recommend this book to that heart who strives to know God and to make him known to the little ones who call her 'momma.' Kimm is a candid and gracious fellow sojourner, faithfully pointing to God's immeasurable steadfast love and grace in the midst of our mess. She helps us peer beyond what our eyes can see to behold the glorious end on which our hearts can rest."

Lauren Chandler, wife of Matt Chandler (pastor of The Village Church), mother of 3, writer, singer and speaker

"What a healing balm this book has been to my heart. In *Christ in the Chaos*, my dear friend Kimm points us to the rest that every mother longs for. This rest that each tired and burdened mom needs is found in the work that Christ has done. Kimm shows us how the gospel changes our motherhood from a drudgery to a joy. She helps us to see that Christ meets us in the middle of our everyday and loves us in the midst of our failures. She gives us the truth of free grace that unshackles us from trying to be the mom of the year. Kimm makes herself small and makes Christ big. I pray each mom who finds this book falls more in love with her Savior and becomes more aware of how his love for her changes everything about her."

Jessica Thompson, Co-author of *Give them Grace*

"Jesus tells us that his yoke is easy and his burden is light. Why, then, as a mom of a rapidly growing family did I feel as if I were carrying the weight of the world and these children on my shoulders alone? I had forgotten the gospel and instead was piling on the 'have-to's' that promised to fulfill me as a wife, give me purpose as a mother, and produce guaranteed spiritual kids. I just wish I had read and absorbed the truths that Kimm so gently reminds us of as mothers: Christ is not only in the chaos, he sees you, loves you, and is beckoning you to rest in the work he has already completed."

Kendra Fletcher, Homeschool mother of eight and blogger at PreschoolersAndPeace.com

"As mothers we are tempted to stack up our maternal achievements as a measure of our godliness. Consider Kimm's book as a megaphone—loud and clear—calling out the better way: Moms need to build their hope on nothing less than Jesus' blood and righteousness. Read this book in the context of community and see how the gospel intersects and powerfully affects the details of your motherhood and friendships."

Gloria Furman, author of *Glimpses of Grace*

"Few people on the planet know chaos better than moms of young children. Wanting everything to be right, safe, and in order, moms know that it rarely is. This easily leads to feelings of fear, guilt, and exasperation. My friend Kimm Crandall lives in the trenches of motherhood and has discovered that chaos can be the perfect context to experience God's liberating grace. She is a wise, practical, gospel-drenched guide for anyone navigating through the wearisome terrain of parenting. I highly recommend this book and hope that it's the first of many from Mrs. Crandall."

Tullian Tchividjian, Pastor of Coral Ridge Presbyterian Church and author of *Glorious Ruin: How Suffering Sets You Free*

"Let's be honest, motherhood — though a great joy — can be quite chaotic. Kimm Crandall, mother of four and author of *Christ in the Chaos*, knows this all too well and wants to encourage us that God is there with us through every sickness, messy room, baseball game, trial, and joy. Kimm had learned to do all the right things like so many Christians do, yet when her performance and good works weren't bringing her joy and contentment, she broke. Part of the chaos of motherhood may not be external at all, but rather an internal chaos produced by striving to be the perfect mom and forgetting our identity in Christ. This identity, as Kimm explains, is rooted in a perfect love for an imperfect mom. Our greatest need as mothers isn't the latest news and trends, our greatest need is Christ. Kimm gently but boldly reminds us that our performance won't sustain us. We need the sweet and gracious mercy and love of God found in the cross of Christ — found in our chaos."

Trillia Newbell, author and editor of *Women of God Magazine*

Table of Contents

CruciformPress
something new in Christian publishing

Our Books: Short. Clear. Concise. Helpful. Inspiring. Gospel-focused. *Print; 3 ebook formats.*

Consistent Prices: Every book costs the same.

Subscription Options: Print books or ebooks delivered to you on a set schedule, at a discount. Or buy print books or ebooks individually.

Pre-paid or Recurring Subscriptions
Print Book	$6.49 each
Ebook	$3.99 each

Non-Subscription Sales
1-5 Print Books	$8.45 each
6-50 Print Books	$7.45 each
More than 50 Print Books	$6.45 each
Single Ebooks (bit.ly/CPebks)	$5.45 each
Bundles of 7 Ebooks	$35.00
Ebook Distribution Program	6 pricing levels

Christ in the Chaos: How the Gospel Changes Motherhood

Print / PDF ISBN:	978-1-936760-70-1
ePub ISBN:	978-1-936760-72-5
Mobipocket ISBN:	978-1-936760-71-8

Published by Cruciform Press, Adelphi, Maryland. Copyright © 2013 by Kimm Crandall. All rights reserved. Unless otherwise indicated, all Scripture quotations are taken from: *The Holy Bible: English Standard Version*, Copyright © 2001 by Crossway Bibles, a division of Good News Publishers. Used by permission. All rights reserved. Italics or bold text within Scripture quotations indicates emphasis added.

FOREWORD

More Than Chaotic Circumstances

It's been quite some time since I had children in my home—at least for more than an evening's sleepover. Yes, I've raised three children, but my youngest is now a 35-year-old father of two. And although I do have six really adorable grandchildren, they don't live with me permanently, and when things get chaotic with them, it's not long until their parents take them home and I breathe a sigh of relief. My "mothering" years are pretty much over and have been for quite some time.

In light of that reality, you might wonder why I'm writing the Foreword to a book for moms in the midst of chaos. After all, with just me and Phil at home now, I wouldn't describe our well-ordered days and quiet evenings as "chaotic." So it may not seem logical for me to write this foreword, but actually it is the most logical thing in the world. That's because even though I don't have the circumstantial chaos of four kids under the age of 10 like Kimm does, I am well acquainted with my own chaotic heart. And I know heart chaos is the result of a worship disorder, not circumstances. We all have that in common, so whether you have two kids or 12, this book will be helpful for you.

You see, a heart in turmoil isn't that way because of circumstances. No, circumstances only push to the forefront what's already there—the chaos hidden in the heart. Heart chaos is a result of the inward worship of self: worship of my own abilities to merit God's favor and approve of myself, the desire to compare my success with others, the longing to know that deep down I'm really okay. Heart chaos comes from thinking that all the goodness in my personal world (especially the salvation of my children and grandchildren) depends on my getting my act together. Chaos is a worship disorder: it results from worship of myself, my abilities, my plans, me. It happens when I believe the lies that if I could just "try harder" and "do better" everything would be okay.

Chaos doesn't turn into peace simply because I've read a book or gone to a seminar. It isn't solved by making concise lists and being able to look at others and know I am finally doing "it" (whatever "it" happens to be—parenting, grandparenting, you name it) right. Chaos turns into peace when the Prince of Peace speaks deeply into your heart and tells you, "Be still. I am God. I've got this."

This is the truth Kimm has learned in the crucible of her own personal chaos. She has struggled with her own heart—a heart that longed to find the key that would make everything, especially her family and by extension her own existence, okay. You might be surprised by her candor. She isn't pretending to be a great mom (though she's a faithful one). She isn't pretending to be sinless (though she loves holiness). And, thankfully, she doesn't give you any helpful hints or long lists of how to be like her. She struggles. She loves. She sins. She repents. She struggles…again. But she has faith in the God who loves sinners and sent his Son to make everything more than okay.

Jesus Christ lived, died, and rose again so parents would know forgiveness for their sins and freedom in righteousness. This book will remind you of that truth—the truth of a Christ who persevered through a furnace of wrath while all he had known deconstructed and became chaos around him. It is all we need to know.

Yes, this book is primarily written for moms, but it really is for anyone—even old grandmas like me. That's because we all need the message of this book: I am a sinner, but I've been loved and welcomed. This message alone will bring peace to my troubled soul. You don't need more "to-do" lists. You don't need to "try harder" or "do better". What you need is for your chaotic heart to remember the gospel.

So read this book. Buy extra copies. Pass them out. Find Christ in your chaos and watch your chaotic heart change.

– Elyse Fitzpatrick

INTRODUCTION

Something odd happens when a woman becomes a mother. The change begins the moment she finds out she is pregnant. It starts within, as her sense of identity shifts. Soon, as if by some irresistible force, books, pamphlets, and coupons of an entirely different kind begin to enter her life. New expectations appear, too. A new mother can spend her entire pregnancy feeling the pressure of eating right, exercising enough, gaining just the right amount of weight, gathering the countless things a baby needs, researching the best way to labor and feed and diaper. The list goes on and on.

Then the baby comes—a beautiful, perfect little bundle of blessing. Somehow, though, within a few days the "mom laws" always show up at the doorstep with a great thud, a massive manual of seemingly non-negotiable do's and don'ts which can crush the spirit of wonder and excitement a new baby brings. Many moms dutifully drag this manual inside, crack it open, and strive to live by its unyielding dictates. I know I did.

In chapter one of the mom manual, we find our identity in the unique chaos of diapers, strollers, and feeding schedules. We arrive at chapter two and live in the world of baby food and play dates. Chapter three covers school pictures and piano lessons. As the book continues, we move through the teen years, on into college and young adulthood. At every turn in our lives, the lesson is relentlessly reinforced: thou shalt not disobey the mom manual. Whether through books, blogs, or even the pressure of other moms (be it spoken or unspoken) it can seem as though life has been reduced to a single standard, one that is both iron-clad yet somewhat vague: the value of our motherhood stands or falls on how well we follow the manual.

The book you now hold in your hands is for moms who sense that the manual is not the last word. Moms who have been beaten down by endless demands to simply "try harder" and "do better." Moms starved of grace. Moms who have been told they must perform to a specific standard if they want to be godly women.

This book is for moms who need to hear how the gospel changes motherhood.

As a mother, I need to hear over and over the good news that Christ came to be my friend when I hated him. (Because some days, it looks like I still do.) I need to hear the good news that he lived a perfect sinless life on my behalf because he knew just how much I would make a mess of things. (Which I do on a regular basis.) He knew at times I would yell at my kids (yes), not desire my husband (it happens), and want to run away screaming (which happens surprisingly often). He knew my doubts and fears, and he knew I could never live a life acceptable to his perfect standard. So he lived … for me.

Jesus lived without ever letting a twinge of impatience color his voice. In crowded settings, he never got annoyed at all of the touching, and he never treated others as less important than himself. But here's where the Christian version of the mom manual so often gets it wrong—Jesus didn't do all this so I could primarily focus on trying harder and asking "What would Jesus do?" every time chaos ensues.

Jesus is not only my example…He is my replacement.

Jesus came to do everything I haven't done and could never do, and he did it sinless and perfectly. Then, he died the perfect death for my righteousness.

Not once did he open his mouth when falsely accused, nor lash out at those who didn't believe. In quietness he was beaten, stripped, and nailed to a beam of wood, and he willingly did it because of my sin. He was the spotless lamb sacrificed for all the polluted filth of my life; I couldn't get clean any other way. He was separated from his Father so he could take on the loads of wrath which my sin deserved. He suffered so there would be no condemnation against me. None!

Jesus served me on the cross by taking my record of sin—all the heinous deeds I would ever commit—and replacing it with the grace gift of his perfect, righteous record so that when God looks at me, he is not disappointed or disgusted but instead says, "This is my beloved daughter with whom I am well pleased, always and forever—not just when she is doing good, and even when she runs from me."

This book is about what that kind of grace looks like for mothers specifically. It's about how Christ gives peace to women laboring under the burden of all those unwritten mom rules. It's about how Christ sets mothers free to love him.

You will find the chapters of this book are sound, but short. To the point, but not heavy—just right for the mom who has been up all night with the baby, the mom who only has a few minutes waiting for the school bus, and for the mom who relishes her own bathroom breaks as an opportunity to read a couple of pages even if her toddler spends the whole time pounding on the door. This book will not weigh you down with another list of things to do but aims to free you by reminding you of what's already been done for you.

Let this book shout "Gospel!" loud and clear over all the noisy, pushy mom laws. The gospel of Jesus Christ is the only thing you need now in the thick of mothering. In fact, it's the only thing you ever need. The gospel will get you through those long nights of newborns crying and those long days of caring for clingy, feverish toddlers. Take the gospel with you on those car trips back and forth from soccer to piano. Let the gospel guide you when you drop your "baby" off at college and he steps forward into young adulthood. Bask in Christ's love for you and bathe in the outrageous grace you receive day-in and day-out no matter how many times you fail: the gospel will help you find Christ in all that goes on within and around you.

My years with children have seen lots of laughter and tears, illness and sweetness, pleasure and pain, depression and joy. Through the chaos and the trials, God has awakened my heart to the good news that he is not mad at me—there is grace for this sinful mother. God has changed me through his gospel, giving me a new love and a new life, and I hope the same thing will happen to you as you read the good news of his grace and mercy in this book.

Are you looking for Christ in your chaos? As you journey through these pages with me, I pray you will begin to see just how much Christ loves you ... in your chaos, too.

One
GOD'S FAITHFULNESS TO MOTHERS

Mumbling through my tears, I confessed to my husband that I had decided there was no God. He had walked into our bedroom and found me in the rocking chair in the corner, crying in the dark. I hadn't slept well for months. I felt desperate and broken. When he asked me what was wrong, it all came pouring out.

Our family had been going through some challenging situations which for me had snowballed into dark days and restless nights. It didn't seem like God was answering our prayers or giving any indication he cared. For months I had struggled with doubt, wondering whether God even existed, yet whenever I admitted this to others whom I admired in the church, they told me, "You just have to have faith," and "You must not be reading your Bible and praying enough. Let me help you figure out a plan for a daily quiet time."

Yeah, right. With a 6-year-old, a 4-year-old, a 2-year-old, and a newborn, my house was anything but quiet. I longed for any brief nap or small moment of relief from the

24-hour cycle of nursing, potty training, and homeschooling. I could barely make it from one day to the next. To be told my struggles must come from not reading my Bible enough or praying the right way?! With great restraint, let me just suggest this advice was far from helpful.

Honestly, I had tried to do it right. I had pushed myself to read God's Word when I didn't understand, and I made myself pray when I didn't want to. I sewed dresses, baked bread, sang hymns, volunteered in the nursery, and read all the right books. I didn't need to "try harder;" I truly *couldn't* try harder, and I couldn't take on one more duty. As it turned out, I couldn't even continue to shoulder what I was already carrying, so I broke. If this is what it meant to be a Christian, then I obviously didn't have what it took. Apparently, other people thought they could do it, but I knew I would only disappoint. Not too long afterward, there I was weeping in my rocking chair, devastated to imagine God couldn't be real after all—the Christian life which had been portrayed to me was clearly far too much for anyone to handle.

Sadly, I know I am not the only mother who has felt the oppressive weight of Christian duty as it is so often and so falsely portrayed. Read your Bible, pray, dress this way, speak that way, and all your dreams will come true. God will be happy and so will you. Your kids will be a blessing and never rebel. You will never trip on your walk with God…unless, of course, you neglect your daily quiet times.

For me, and maybe even for you, really devastating things happened after we entered into the family of God. Yes, much in those early days was astonishing and glorious and wonderful. But a few months or years later, depending on your resiliency and your particular church environment, your shine started to dull and your love began to wane. The newness was no longer new, and most of the amazement and wonder had left the building. What then? If you're like me, you moved right along to the list of Christian duties that more "mature" saints had been pressing you about since that first day.

It's true, isn't it? Shamefully, I confess that after crossing that maturity threshold, I myself helped put younger Christians into prisons of guilt, self-righteousness, and joyless perfectionism. I couldn't see it at the time, but I was really just urging them to come join me in the prison cell where I already lived.

My Initiation into Doing the Right Thing

I can't pinpoint when I was saved. I'm not even sure when I discovered Jesus. But I can tell you exactly when I discovered church, and how I learned to look and smell "like a Christian." So when I think back on my early years as a believer, I can clearly see why I struggled with assurance of my salvation: I had it all backwards. Before my heart was in love with Jesus, I tried to make my feet, hands, and lips do Christian work. I put my faith in my own ability to express faith, not in salvation through the grace God had given me.

When I was 15, I participated in a winter camp with my sister's youth group. Periodically throughout the day, we would break into small groups for study and reflection. As we sat in our circles of eight or so, each of us feeling awkward and wishing we'd move on to the fun stuff, the teacher would often ask about our testimonies. Moving in order around the circle, the answers to the question, "When did you become a Christian?" were consistently pretty generic—something about winter camp or a summer backpacking trip where a group of friends goes forward together during an altar call. Waiting my turn, I easily formulated my answer in my head: "I have been a Christian since I was born." I completely believed it. After all, I had always believed in God, and that's what these people were talking about, right? My turn finally came and I was ready, awkwardness and all. Here we go!

That's when the group leader skipped me. Skipped right over me to the next person, like I wasn't there. Only me.

The weekend went on and I sang the songs, prayed when I was supposed to, and started learning about the external behaviors of a "good Christian." It all seemed easy enough—I didn't have any interest in drinking or smoking, and the whole boy thing wasn't happening for me anyway. Walking the "Christian" walk didn't seem too different from what I already knew.

As the final meeting came to a close, the leader of our group pulled me aside and asked if I wanted to pray with her. My compliant, people-pleasing self agreed. After all, praying is what these people did, and they had given me much practice in the preceding days. As I bowed my head, she asked me to repeat after her. I did exactly that. Words went into my ears in her voice and came out of my mouth in my voice, without ever stopping for even an instant to check in with my mind or heart. When I got to "Amen" she proclaimed me a Christian. This confused me a little because I had thought I was a Christian already, but she apparently understood these mysteries, so I went with it.

That prayer did change things, however. It initiated me into a new club with all new friends—nice kids with somewhat good manners who never made me feel bad for not wanting to drink, smoke, or have sex. When the leader proclaimed, "Kimm is now a Christian," I received countless hugs and congratulations.

Of course, the next natural step in my "initiation" was baptism. The pressure felt tremendous, and I wanted to comply, but my parents thought I should wait until I was 18 to make sure I was mature enough to make the decision. This was one of the only times I can remember not getting what I requested from my parents, and I was actually glad about it. What self-conscious 15-year-old really wants to get dunked under water and come up sopping wet with her hair plastered to her head in front of the boy she likes?

Even without being baptized, however, I was still accepted in the youth group. Wanting to stay that way, I started learning the rules. I began to have faith in this new way of living which seemed to promise a kind of general happiness. Sundays took on a whole new excitement for me. No more was it just a boring day hanging around the house with my parents—I now had something to do and immediately began attending Sunday school, morning service, evening church, and every single youth group activity. The games were fun, the snacks were great, and, most of all, I belonged. I felt set for life.

My Failing Faith in Doing the Right Thing

Throughout high school, I continued attending retreats and camps, re-dedicating my life to Christ each time; I went to youth conferences and walked forward for each altar call to proclaim I would be a better Christian from then on. All the "good Christians" did these things, and I was the type of kid who only did what I could do well, so I worked hard at following the pattern set before me. It seemed like you could never be too serious about becoming (and re-becoming) a "good Christian."

When the age of 18 came, I was dunked. I don't remember any feelings from that day besides enjoying the extra attention I received. So baptism came and went. Thereafter, my faithfulness during college depended on which boy I was dating and what sport I was playing at the time. Sometimes I mustered up fire for Jesus, and other times I stayed away from Christian activities because I didn't want to hear that making out with boys or missing church to participate in horseshows was bad. If I didn't look the part at the moment, I would just stay away. The church had taught me about being a good witness, and that wasn't my profile, so why would they want an imperfect soul like mine around?

Once I was married and began my journey into motherhood, I began to question my salvation as my faithfulness to God grew burdensome and uninteresting. As a young wife and mother, it seemed truly impossible to continue what I called a "faithful walk with God," and I began to break down. I couldn't sleep well. Illness and depression set in. Yet a glimmer of God's unending mercy shined through, and I saw I had lived far too long in works-based righteousness, putting my faith in my own faithfulness, trying to earn my favor with God. I had depended on my own works and whether people around me accepted me. I had left Jesus behind in my pursuit of being a good Christian.

Not until God stripped away my faith in "doing the right thing" did I begin to see how much effort I had put into living a life according to the law. I couldn't take the pressure of my own self-righteousness anymore, but the message from the pulpit and from others in the church always seemed the same: "try harder" to please God. Once I got honest and confessed my practical atheism—the opening scene from this chapter—I dove into a year of darkness during which God stripped away every façade. After that, I could finally marvel at just how much Christ had done for me. I could see the outrageous grace he had given me by sending his Son to earn my salvation. Only when I saw the insufficiency of all the hope I had put in myself could I truly see his faithfulness.

What Do You Make of That?

I've analyzed my salvation story over and over. I've pored over old journals looking for evidence of a change within my heart. But I cannot pinpoint anything and can only trust that God knows when my heart changed. The important thing is that I know *now* my faith does not depend on my own works but rests in the completed work of Jesus Christ who has saved me.

What disturbs me is how much the earlier part of my story resembles the present reality of so many Christians in the Church today. Their assurance of salvation hinges on how they answer the question, "What and how much are you doing for God?" rather than what they confess and believe about the gospel (Romans 10:9). Countless opportunities to go forward and proclaim, "Today, I stop sinning and start acting like a Christian!" will only obscure the gospel and breed a works-based "try harder" and "do better" brand of Christianity. Where the gospel is not the beginning, middle, and end of the salvation message, all you really have is another social club with initiation rites and a code of conduct.

Of course, Christianity *does* have a kind of code, but God did not give his law because he expects us to complete it. He gave it to crush our spirits into understanding that if we are not rescued from our inability to do everything required, we will suffer the wrath of God. He never meant for anyone except Jesus Christ to check off each item on that list, but Jesus did exactly that. He fulfilled the law, once and for all, in order to set us free from it.

I was recently asked how I know God is faithful. Many of us could easily say how God has blessed us with friends and family, a home in a free country, and a Bible in every room. But God's faithfulness is not measured by tangible blessings. It's measured by his character and his promises to us. Yes, things around me obviously signal his goodness to me—I am grateful for my family, my husband's job, and food on the table, but I hope I would still know God is real and faithful even without those things. If we lost our home, if our children became unthinkably rebellious, or if we became sick with cancer, would we still feel so confident in his faithfulness?

So how do I know God is faithful? Because in the year that I denied my faith in Christ, he never let me go. My depression never consumed me, and though I continued to run from God and push him away, nothing moved the Lord away from me. In his kindness, he broke me to the point of near nothingness, and then he showed me his relentless faithfulness.

God was faithful in sending his Son just as the angel had promised Mary (Luke 1:30-33). Jesus, in turn, was faithful in fulfilling the law on our behalf (Matthew 5:17). He is faithful to take our place in God's judgment (1 John 4:10). He is faithful to remain in us through his Spirit (John

14:16-17). If our triune God was faithful to do all of this for us, will he not remain faithful to us today?

What can be so hard to understand in our prideful self-reliance is that God's promise to remain faithful is entirely one-sided. He hasn't told us that if we are good and do all the right things, *then* he will never leave us. No, he has given us the gift of the Holy Spirit to live inside of us and affirm that we belong to the Father (Galatians 4:6). His Spirit will never throw up his hands and declare that we are just too difficult to live with and float away in a huff.

Despite all my confusion, doubts, and unbelief, God has reminded me that nothing can separate me from his love. Satan has tried to use my goodness, my commitment to doing the right things, my badness in gross sin, my doubts, and my unbelief to separate me from the love of God, but I have complete confidence that his goal is impossible (Romans 8:35-39).

God's Unfailing Mercy to Moms

Be honest with yourself. Are you delighting in Christ with the same child-like enthusiasm you had the day you started this walk? Or has your skip through the fields of freedom turned into a trudge up the hill of duty? If it has, do you know why? Because you left Jesus behind. We often act as if he was merely our ticket in—the bouncers at the door wanted proof you were with him, but once they let you pass through, you ditched the One who saved your soul and moved on to greater acts of service. Or so you thought.

My friend, this is not uncommon. If you have left Jesus in your pursuit of becoming a "good Christian," then you will struggle in your faith and assurance of salvation. So return to your faith in God's abundant grace, which he poured out on you through the gospel of Jesus Christ.

My life looks much different today than it did that dark morning in the rocking chair. God has rebuilt my faith in his amazing grace for me as a wretched sinner, and I have abandoned my faith in "doing the right thing" because I now understand that my efforts to be a "good Christian" cannot and will not bring me any more favor than I already have with my Father. I also know that my days as a "bad Christian" do not shatter my status as his daughter. My performance as a churchgoer and wife and mother cannot earn or destroy my Father's affections because Christ has already performed perfectly on my behalf. My Father is just as pleased with me in my darkest hours, wondering if he's really there, as when I have served him faithfully. My God is an always-faithful, never-changing God for this always-changing mom.

Getting Real

1. Our testimonies can tell us a lot about where we have really put our faith. Write a short summary of your personal testimony to share with others.
2. What do you think makes someone a "good Christian?" Why?
3. What do you find yourself putting your faith in today? Does the hope you have in your parenting, marriage, or ministry override your hope in the finished work of Christ? What does it mean to really "rest" in Christ?
4. What assures you of your salvation? Are you afraid that if your commitment to God waivers, then he will drop his commitment to you? What does 2 Timothy 2:13 tell us about God's faithfulness?

Two

AN IDENTITY OTHER THAN "MOM"

You might say my 8-year-old son has identity issues.

Last winter he was a basketball player. He wore the shoes, watched the games, and announced he would go "pro" someday. When spring came with its dewy mornings of fresh-cut grass and little boys in crisp uniforms excited to play America's pastime, my son ate, drank, and slept baseball. He poured himself into learning players' names. He would watched the games on TV fully dressed in his uniform, holding a vacuum nozzle as his bat and a couch pillow for his base. He slept in his uniform and even wore it to school—cup and everything.

Over the summer we spent time each week at the beach. And what do you know? He wanted to be a surfer. Convinced he was good enough to be a professional, he started petitioning me for a board. He even complained that the waves weren't good enough and that we needed to go elsewhere to catch better ones. I smiled and nodded.

By this time it's fall and, as you can guess, my son's new passion is football. He has been practicing all the moves and watching all the games. He wore four shirts out of the house one night because he wanted to look like he was wearing pads.

In between all of this, my little guy is a cowboy too. He longs to rope a steer so he dons a hat, jeans, belt, and boots…but only when his best friend is around.

Obviously, from pro-athlete to surfer to cowboy, the boy is trying to find himself.

I'm not too concerned for him, as I know this is a normal childhood thing. But it reminds me how I can get caught up in trying to find my identity as well.

What Kind of Mom Am I?

I remember telling a friend last year how I was struggling with some of these issues. I could see I was on the brink of a "season shift"— leaving the season of babies, naps, and play dates for a season of busy school days and extracurricular activities. I was feeling a little insecure, unsure of my new status because it all seemed so unfamiliar.

When I first became a mother, I decided to claim a few identities as my own. I was going to be a "quiverfull, all-natural, homeschooling, dress-wearing, bread-baking, whole-foods-eating mother." Then the babies came. And came and came and came. That was it. I couldn't be the kind of mother I wanted to be—the kind of woman I honestly regarded as more godly than others. So I labeled myself a failure and spent the next several years in a terrible depression. Yes, years.

The realm of motherhood has many subcategories. There is the homeschool mom, the working mom, the mom of many, the PTA mom, the soccer mom…the list goes on and on, and you can find blogs and support groups for each one of them. But is that all you are? Does your ultimate worth depend on how you enact your motherhood? Quite frankly, the thought of finding all my value in the fact that I bore children just puts me in the "depressed mom" category. And that's exactly where I was until I came to understand my real identity in Christ.

Have you ever stopped to think about your self-labels? How do you categorize yourself? In what "me role" do you truly belong? You may be tempted to say, "Well, I know who I am: God's child!" That's a nice Sunday school answer, but are you living there? Does this truth stir anything in you on those days when you are drowning in laundry, dishes, and bickering kids? Where does this truth fit in with your everyday life?

Remembering Who I Am

It seems clear to me that the Lord designed all my challenges so I would eventually turn to him and learn where my true identity is hidden: in Christ. Sometimes the busyness of life becomes all a mom really thinks about—the to-do list runs your days and you see yourself in terms of all the mundane things you do. Or maybe you never had an accurate view of what it really means to be in Christ. If you are a busy Christian mother, you must guard your heart. Fight against forgetting who you are in Jesus, lest you come down like I did with a bad case of what Elyse Fitzpatrick calls "spiritual amnesia":

> ...too many of us are suffering from spiritual amnesia; an amnesia that has obscured our true identity as it's been defined by the gospel....Even though we believe the gospel, the occasions in which the gospel (the

incarnation, sinless life, death, bodily resurrection, and ascension of the Son of God) actually intersect and powerfully affect our daily life are infrequent.[1]

I spiraled into depression because I had forgotten who I was as a saved, forgiven believer. I was living a life of trying harder to "do better," thinking that I needed to earn my right standing with God. At the time, I probably wouldn't have used those words to explain myself, but that was exactly the logic driving my actions. Instead, what I really needed was for the gospel to "intersect and powerfully affect" the details of my everyday life.

Check yourself to see whether your identity is in the gospel or something else: every thought and every action is fueled by your sense of identity. Take for instance one Friday night when I went to bed with an agenda: I had decided that because I am a "busy mom" who had to wake up before six o'clock nearly every morning, I deserved to sleep in on that particular Saturday. That sense of identity controlled my thoughts about myself and also the actions I planned to take.

Around 6:30 the following morning, one of the kids knocked on my door with a question. This was followed by three more visits from different children and several more from the first child. Each time the door opened my warm, dark bedroom was flooded with blinding light. Things were not going as I'd wanted; people were not falling neatly into line where I had placed them in my head. Eventually I rolled out of bed well before I wanted to—but not before some harsh words escaped my lips, and not before I had given myself a new label, already the second one in a brand-new day. I was now the selfish, guilty mom.

How quickly my sense of self had changed! Over the course of just 30 minutes, I had allowed my sinful and selfish actions to completely redefine me in my own eyes.

I showered and dressed, trying hard to push the selfishness of my heart to the side and change my status from "selfish mom" to "mom extraordinaire." That was the answer—I just needed a fresh sense of self, a little personal pep talk. In order to live up to my newly-declared status, I decided to slip smoothly into my superhero suit by making special pancakes for the family. Surely this kind of serving was the opposite of selfish, right?

As I mixed and flipped pancakes and prepared the coffee, I grew more and more agitated with my 4-year-old's whining and the other kids' bickering. Couldn't they see I was doing something nice for them? With every sigh, every threatening look, and every complaint to my husband, I was losing my bid for "mom extraordinaire."

With breakfast eaten and the dishes cleared, I began to realize how off-base my self-interpretation was. I had conducted my morning as if my performance would earn me acceptance, not only with my family but with my God. I found my worth in who I imagined I was—first as "busy mom" who believed she deserved 30 more minutes of quiet sleep, then as "selfish mom" who spent those 30 minutes agitated with her children, then as "mom extraordinaire" who thought she could make up for it all by orchestrating a perfect morning for her family. But I had completely forgotten who I was in Christ. I had forgotten my worth is only in what Jesus has done for me. My identity is in him, not in my busyness or my sleepiness or my cooking skills.

At that very moment in my kitchen, I repented and reminded myself just how great God's love for me is. Then I saw again that my status as his daughter never changes, even when I throw a fit because I don't get my way. I saw again that I do not need to earn the "daughter" label because it has already been earned for me through Christ's blood—in fact, I cannot earn that status at all. I saw again who I am in Christ: loved, forgiven, and righteous. I was freed from striving to be "mom extraordinaire." And only then could I rest in my right standing with God through his Son.

Did this make my children instantly behave better? Did it make me feel like I had gotten more sleep? Did it erase the tension I had added to our home with my unkindness? Not really. But it did give me rest in my soul. It reminded me that my sins of that morning had been forgiven at the cross; and that the future of my children ultimately rests in God's hands (not mine); and that the Father works all things for my good. I discovered the Holy Spirit is with me and in me no matter how many times I veer wildly from one faulty self-image to another.

If you are a mother, you are in a wonderful yet consuming season in your life. But the fact that you are a mother does not make you who you are. Nor does your worth as a person reflect your skill or delight (or lack thereof) in mothering. Rather, your true identity comes from who you are in Christ.

Two Gifts: No Guilt and Total Righteousness

So who are you in Christ? At the moment you were saved, he gave you two gifts that completely redefined your identity. The first was having your slate wiped clean. You immediately had no record of wrongs against you because every sin you ever did or will commit was laid upon Jesus and paid for. Your guilt was erased, leaving you clean, pure, and acceptable before God, and this is still true today—no matter what.

But wait—it gets better! Not only did God delete from your account everything that should have counted against you, he then chose to give you the gift of righteousness through his Son. At the moment of your salvation, the infinitely perfect and utterly comprehensive righteousness the Son had (and has) before the Father was counted as yours—forever! "For if, because of one man's trespass, death reigned through that one man, much more will those who receive the abundance of grace and the free gift of righteousness reign in life through the one man Jesus Christ" (Romans 5:17). The perfect, sinless obedience of Jesus makes your shameful, polluted disobedience disappear, and then he fills in your record with his perfect righteousness. You do not get a fresh, clean slate so you can start over—you would only mess it all up again in no time! Instead, your slate is wiped clean so it can now display the perfect record of our Savior!

It seems many Christians, myself included, find it hard to remember the second gift. Told that our slate is now clean, we rejoice. But then our follow-through is all wrong—we assume that, having been given a clean slate, our job now is to go forth, produce good fruit, do lots of good works, and try really hard to keep a perfectly God-honoring record. It is often suggested to us—and often we assume—that if we mess up we have to start all over. We think that if we mess up our slate is marred or even ruined, and then we have to prove we deserve to have it wiped clean again.

There are two assumptions hidden in that impression. Both of them are completely wrong.

First, our slate is perfect because it contains the perfect righteousness of Jesus credited to us. I don't care how bad a mom or a wife or a woman you are—if you are a Christian your sin cannot change what Jesus did at the cross for you. And it cannot erase the fact that God has credited his Son's perfect righteousness to you.

Second, you didn't do anything to deserve having your slate wiped clean to begin with. So, even if you could mess it up, you would never be able to earn its return to perfection.

So, how has your day been? How about your month, or your year, or your last decade? Sporadic faithfulness? Frustrating battles with sin that are never completely won? The amazing good news is that your record before the Father is still perfect! It has been perfect since the very moment of your salvation, and it will be perfect even when you stand before him.

By his own sacrifice, Jesus has thrown your sin away as far as the east is from the west (Psalm 103:12), and he gives you as a free gift his righteous record. No more striving: Jesus has already pleased his Father completely on your behalf.

This beautiful truth can bring you endless freedom. It may seem hard to believe—your reasonable self may want to reject it as an insane act of grace. Indeed, God's grace is too outrageous, too impossible to comprehend, but that's exactly how we know it completely destroys our "try harder" and "do better" law. God's grace leaves us with nothing of ourselves but all of Jesus.

As mothers, we can go forward confident in the truth that our identity rests in the perfect and righteous record given to us by Christ. We have nothing to prove—no status to live up to—because Christ proved it all on the cross. He has given us the ultimate status: we are "perfect mom" through his blood. Preach this truth to yourself when things start to unravel, when you begin grasping for control by snapping at the kids or belittling your husband. Remind yourself how much you have been loved, and delight in the grace which then floods in—the presence of God in your chaos.

Getting Real

1. What category of "mom" do you most identify with?
2. According to Colossians 3:3 ("For you have died, and your life is hidden with Christ in God"), where is your true identity found? What is the purpose in understanding your true identity? Why should you care?
3. What does this statement (from earlier in the chapter) mean: "Every thought and every action is fueled by your sense of identity"? Do you agree with this statement? Why or why not?
4. Share one example of how understanding your true identity in Christ has played out in your daily life.

Three

GOD'S LOVE FOR MOTHERS

"Pick up your shoes in the hallway."

"No, put the toothbrush down."

"What do you mean you don't have the stuff to take care of your braces?"

"You forgot a shoe."

"Boys, go to bed...*now*!"

"That story's too long. I'm too tired for a long story. We're reading this one."

"That shoe is still in the hallway!"

"No, I don't know where your CD is."

"Please give your sister the CD out of your stereo."

"Stop crying."

"Justin! Can you get the girls settled?"

"Why did you take your sister's CD?"

"What's that smell? Whoa, what is going on with these shoes?"

"Good night. I love you."

That's a fairly typical bedtime at our house with four children 10 and under. Exhausted, not wanting to serve anyone but myself, I react and rush and demand.

I manage the chaos and do the routine, sometimes sweetly and sometimes not. I read to the kids, but often quickly and in a monotone. I sing "Jesus Loves Me" because it's what we've done since they were babies. I do love them, but this seems like the best I can do with all of their needs and complaints when I've been up since 4:30 a.m. It's not a perfect love; it's *my* love. It's what my kids know of their weak and sinful mom.

Some evenings I put the kids to bed and am soon overcome by tears of guilt and shame. I imagine that, because of my sin, my children must feel so unloved, and that I must not be good enough because I love them so imperfectly. Other evenings I put them to bed and pat myself on the back, thinking what a great mom I just was and basking in the artificial glow of my self-righteousness.

Two kinds of evenings, same problem. Whether I'm lamenting my imperfections or celebrating my Awesome Mom-ness, in each case I have forgotten my righteous standing in Christ. And either way, my love is tainted. It's tainted with the sin of selfish desires, pride, and so much more. As much as I long to have perfect love for my children, and as much as I sometimes deceive myself into thinking I have exactly that, my love is never perfect. My love for my children comes from a heart in constant battle with sin. As often as I repent, my bedtime technique will always suffer from an unloving motive somewhere in my heart.

Christ has good news for me, though: I don't have to despair, even at my repeated failures—because my identity is not "a loving mom." Instead, as we saw in the last chapter, my identity is rooted in the righteousness I have in Christ. Yes, every child needs a loving mom, but the only way I can move forward from failure and love my children well is if I find my identity in what Christ has already given me. Then, and only then, can I begin to love them with his love.

Abiding Love for a Lonely Mom

The Lord made this clear to me during a trip I took a couple of years ago. Walking into the airport by myself, it took only moments to begin missing my family. Yet at the same time what I wanted most was to savor a few minutes with no responsibilities, no questions to answer, and no one to mother. So I decided to sit down right there in the airport lobby, choosing the only red chair in a long line of black chairs. It made me feel special.

As a toddler screamed nearby, I thought about the night before. My little girl had clung to me at dinner, crying and begging me not to leave. Her big brother had come over to console her but then burst into tears at her sadness. This was the last straw for my big girl who had been valiantly holding her emotions in check, at least until the dam burst. My littlest guy sat there at the table and laughed at us all. He didn't get it. To him it was just another bit of the sweet chaos that blankets our days. And over the heads of my clinging children I caught the eye of my husband who was sitting in silent angst of what the weekend would hold for him as a single parent.

Normally I would have been excited about going away on a trip; it doesn't happen much. But this time was different. My kids knew I was going to see Grandma, and they knew Grandma was sick. They could see in my tired face I was not going joyfully. They had heard me tell others about her cancer. They longed to see her and Grandpa too.

On the plane, I sat directly behind that same screaming toddler, and he was still at it. I wanted to give the parents grace—I have often been the mom no one wants to sit by—but I had to pray hard not to react. I had felt special in my red chair in the lobby, but now I just wanted distance from noisy children and exhausted parents. I complained silently in self-pity: Didn't anyone care how difficult this trip was going to be for me? Didn't anyone care about my longing for some TLC?

I felt lonely and disregarded, another steer in the cattle car. I questioned whether God really loved me. I asked God to show himself to me, to show me where he was amid the real stuff of life. Where was his love for me when my unbelieving mother had cancer? Where was his love for me when I longed to be home with my husband and children?

That night I sat on the edge of the guest bed in my parents' home, exhausted and lonely as I thought about how over the years I had failed to love my mother and father like I should have. I longed for a hug from my husband and someone to help me sort out my feelings. I texted my husband. I emailed a friend. I checked Facebook. The same old things I have done time after time in search of comfort. The same old things that only provide distraction, and no real comfort at all.

I can't remember how I found the verse. It was almost as if it just appeared. Maybe I was occupying myself with writing and needed a verse on love, or maybe I had actually begun reading my Bible for encouragement. Regardless, what happened next has etched a permanent place in my heart.

Jesus met me in that quiet, lonely room at the end

of an upstairs hallway. He spoke to me and loved me through this very verse: "As the Father has loved me, so have I loved you. Abide in my love" (John 15:9).

Perfect Love for an Imperfect Mom

I know I had read John 15:9 at least a dozen times before. It's right there smack in the middle of John's "true vine" chapter. But when the Holy Spirit illuminated it for me that night, he shined a light on all of my questions about God's love for me.

We know God loves his Son perfectly; it's impossible for him not to. God in his sinless, flawless, holy deity *must* love the sinless, flawless, holy Son perfectly. Imagine what kind of a love that must be! It certainly isn't like the love I had shown my parents or others over the years. Not one of us has ever loved anyone else perfectly. It's not possible. Not even close. Yet in John 15:9, Jesus tells us that he loves us with the same kind of sinless and perfect love that the Father has for him. This seems too good to believe.

Then Jesus follows this mind-blowing declaration with an equally amazing command: "Abide in my love." Live in my love, he says. Dwell in my love. Reside in my love. Remain in my love. My perfect, flawless, eternal, unchanging love. He doesn't tell me to work hard to earn his love or that I had better be grateful someone like him loves me like he does. No, he tells me in the preceding verses that I have been joined to him like fruit to a vine (John 15:4-5). He was comforting the disciples and wanted them to know how very much he loved them; he knew they needed to see that although he was leaving them for a time, he was so intricately woven into them that their union could not be broken. There is no greater intimacy than complete union like that, sharing the same nutrients and the same life-giving source with another.

We have been joined to Christ from the moment God rescued us from ourselves, and through the Holy Spirit we will remain so joined until we go to be with him. There is no end to God's love for us. No break, no interruption, not even a tiny hiccup. Nothing can separate us from God's love: "For I am sure that neither death nor life, nor angels nor rulers, nor things present nor things to come, nor powers, nor height nor depth, nor anything else in all creation, will be able to separate us from the love of God in Christ Jesus our Lord" (Romans 8:38-39).

I misunderstood this verse for a long time. I thought it implied I had to remain faithful in my love for God—that unfailing faithfulness was my job. But no, these verses take a very different angle on God's love by telling me nothing can ever pry its way into my union with Christ. That kind of love and that kind of comfort settles me into loving him more and more, wanting to worship him through prayer, singing, and obedience. That kind of comfort keeps me going because I know I don't have to live as if Jesus will leave me if I make a wrong move.

We cannot fully comprehend God's love, nor can our meager words fully define it. But from what I understand of it now, I know it is a love I cannot escape. It is a love that follows me out to the car when I have blown up at my family and want to run away. It is a love that taps me on the shoulder when I am basking in my "good mom" identity—as though I don't need Christ's righteousness, as though I have somehow come up with my own. It is a love that pursues me and settles me and continues to transform every bit of me into the very image of Christ.

Steady Love for a Busy Mom

When I try to do life on my own, even my love for my children becomes all about my performance—whether I am doing it right or wrong. But when I understand God's love for me, I can begin to love others with motives formed by the gospel rather than by my own impure desires. I can love them with the love of God. Just as 1 John 4:19 says, "We love because he first loved us." The *because* in this verse is important. As it turns out, I cannot love anyone well apart from understanding God's love for me and then acting according to his power at work in me.

Have you ever stopped to think about the nature of God's love for you? Maybe it's something you have always heard about but have not really understood. Maybe the busyness of motherhood along with a misplaced identity have shoved those truths to a back burner. That's exactly why you need to spend some time contemplating God's love for you. Will you meditate on the verses mentioned in this chapter (which are only a small sample of how richly the Bible describes God's love for his children) and replant yourself—or root yourself for the first time—in the reality of God's love? (John 15:9, John 15:4-5, Romans 8:38-39, 1 John 4:19, Zephaniah 3:17)

My little girl told me something profound one day. She said most Christians know that God loves them but don't really know what it means. It was then that she broke into "gospel hands." You know the kind of hands a preacher uses when he is excited? It's a gesture I recently realized I use only when talking about the gospel. Apparently, I passed this down to my eldest child. Once the hands were going, she proceeded to break it down for me like this:

> GOD—the most awesome and cool being in the universe.
> LOVES—thinks you're the coolest thing on earth, even though it doesn't always feel like it.
> YOU—an awesomely loved sinner.

What an amazing observation my 10-year-old had made. She may not fully understand what it means, but she sees the void that each of us has, and she sees that only God can fill it. As God's children we need to swim in the love God pours out on us. Are you doing swan dives, cannonballs, and back flips into his pool of grace and mercy? Or do you timidly dip your toe in, afraid to get your feet wet? How else can we abide in his love than by completely and joyfully immersing ourselves in this most wonderful, gracious gift—a love so infinite it can only come as a gift from God?

God's love for *his* children is not like the sin-tainted love I have for *my* children! It is a pure love. A love that has never known sin. A spotless, faultless, sacrificial, and perfect love. A love that causes God to rejoice over his children with gladness, and exult over us with loud singing (Zephaniah 3:17). I want to love my children as my heavenly Father loves me, but I cannot even begin to do that if I do not understand and rest in his love. His love quiets me and saves me (see Zephaniah 3:17 again) from all my other striving.

Being a mother can be a thankless job. If you look for love and approval in that job from anyone other than

Christ you will soon grow tired and burdened. Jesus accomplished *for* you everything God demands *of* you—this is why God's love toward you is truly unconditional! If you don't fully grasp that, you will go about your days thinking you need to "try *harder*" to "do *better*" in order to *earn* something—when that something is what you already have in Christ! You will focus on your failures and your accomplishments instead of resting in the completed work of Christ—the truth that fuels you to go on serving.

So go on! Jump in, get your hair wet, and let God's love splash you in the face and awaken you to live in the gospel. This is good news!

Getting Real

1. Do you feel as if you are swimming in the pool of God's love for you or are you just merely dipping your toe in? What do you think is holding you back?

2. Think of a time in your life when God revealed his love to you in a special way. How has this encouraged you to love others more?

3. How do each of the following verses help you to see God's great love for you? What other verses can you add to this list?
   - John 15:9-11
   - Romans 8:38-39
   - 1 John 4:19
   - Zephaniah 3:17

Four
DISCOVERING GRACE

I was going to start this chapter with a nice little story about how my favorite librarian always erases my fines, even when I haven't bothered to check under the couch for lost library books. I thought about telling you how she has always erased those fines as an act of mercy and has then bestowed grace on me by allowing me to continue to check out thirty more books when I clearly don't deserve to do so. In fact, because she has been so forgiving, I am motivated to take better care of library books. Thus, I planned on wrapping up my story by likening her niceness toward me, an undeserving library patron who continually loses borrowed material, to the goodness of my God.

But is grace really that tame?

No! Grace doesn't even *begin* to compare to the library lady's moral goodness toward me. Grace is a lion whose roar shakes the ground beneath my feet: scary and dangerous. And grace is a mystery so disturbing I can't bring myself to look away. In fact, I can't help but inch closer because I want a better look. I want to prove it wrong and label it as defective. I want to send it back. How could a holy and just God give me a gift of such complete perfection and forgiveness through his Son? Why would he? It doesn't make sense.

But somehow as I draw near to God's grace—somehow in all the confusion, wonder, and ridiculousness—I fall in love. Not in a sweet, tender, cautious way, but like a kid loudly opening great presents. That's what grace does. It transforms quiet patrons of creation into blubbering, joy-filled maniacs. Grace makes me want to pump my fist into the sky and yell, "Right on, God!" The impossibility of it all makes my hands fly when I start talking about it. Grace moves me.

Grace Makes You God's Friend

Grace is God's declaration to a believer that she can never disappoint him. How could I not be encouraged by that fact? My God will never say, "You've done this umpteen thousand times, and I'm through with you." Instead, because I am "in Christ Jesus" (see Romans 3:24 and Ephesians 2:7-8 for starters), I have been adopted into the family of God and given the perfect righteousness of Jesus, so God looks at me and says, "That's her! That's my daughter. Isn't she so beautiful and perfect?"

When I find it hard to believe God still loves me when I fail, Romans 5:10 brings comfort: "For if while we were enemies we were reconciled to God by the death of his Son, much more, now that we are reconciled, shall we be saved by his life." I can be sure that a God who was committed enough to me to pursue me and love me into his presence— while I was his enemy—will never turn his back on me, now his beloved daughter, right when I need him most.

We need God most when we are bogged down in sin—and Christ died to free us from the curse of sin. Of course God will be there to help us! God's irrevocable commitment to us was proven at the cross, so we know his love for us is immovable and his grace for us is constant.

On the flip side, grace means I can do absolutely nothing to please God more than just being who I am in Christ. Yes, our works are good—they help others and honor God. It is for the sake of such works that we remain in these bodies. But our works are simply a means of living out the standing God has granted us, by grace, through Christ's sacrifice. The works flow *from* the grace, they don't produce the grace. Grace is what saved us and grace is what continues to sustain us—our works don't save *or* sustain. Paul addresses this in Ephesians 2:8-9, writing "For it is by grace that you have been saved through faith. And this is not your own doing; it is the gift from God, not a result of works, so that no one may boast." Good works are not about proving anything or earning anything. They are an act of worship from a heart overwhelmed by what Christ has done.

This is why grace excites me. It makes me want to get up and dance! But how about you? Are you reading this with a blank stare? I want to draw you in to my dance circle, but I won't pull you by the arm. In fact, I can't. The Holy Spirit alone has the power to move you. At best, my words can only deliver the good news.

If you glazed past those paragraphs about God's grace and wonder what all the fuss is about, right now would be the time to stop reading and pray. Ask the Holy Spirit to move in your heart and open your eyes, especially freeing you to read the story I am about to share with you without finger-pointing judgment. The story might shock you, but I want God to use it to show you the power of his grace. Grace is not just nice or even amazing. It's outrageous, and we must meet it with a sense of open desire and expectation.

Grace Makes You Bold

Now, are you ready? Let's read a story about how grace played out in one mom's mess:

A mom puts her little girl on a horse that has already tried to buck her off. She pressures her daughter to do more, and in an instant, her little girl is thrown from the horse's back. Scared and hurting, she lands in a heap in the dirt. The mom checks for broken bones and blood and then callously demands the girl get up and stop crying. When she will not, the mom gets on the horse and runs him up and down the ring trying to get him to buck with her, all the while yelling profanity at the horse in front of her 10-year-old daughter.

This mom has snapped. Her anger is out of control. The pressure of being that "good mom" and doing all the right things for her children has gotten to her. She finally puts the horse away, throws the saddle on the ground, and locks herself in the tack room of the barn to be alone. She feels ashamed by her actions and can't face her family.

After some time and good conversation with a friend, the mom sees how the gospel speaks to her situation. She sees her actions as a window to the depths of her heart. She also sees how they are nothing new under the sun—her God has seen this kind of thing before, in her and in others.

She doesn't have to punish herself or try to make things right by working harder. She thanks God for showing her how weak she is. She runs to him and finds forgiveness. She is doused with a scandalous heap of grace.

She goes to her little girl and asks for forgiveness as well. She tells her how mommy is a great sinner who has a great Savior. She gives her little girl a powerful picture, not of a well-mannered mommy who loves perfectly but of a mommy who needs Jesus and who is loved by Jesus unconditionally.

What if I told you that the mother in this story was me? Does that make you cringe? Have I lost your respect?

That's okay.

You may wonder how I can share this humiliating moment, this private and ugly scene, with the perfect strangers who I hope will read this book. The answer is that I have no shame because Christ has covered that day with grace, and that grace has set me free to admit I am weak.

When Jesus told Paul, "My grace is sufficient for you, for my power is made perfect in weakness" (2 Corinthians 12:9), Paul concluded that no matter what happened, he was not only content to be weak but would even boast in his weaknesses, "so that the power of Christ may rest upon me…. For when I am weak, then I am strong" (2 Corinthians 12:9b-10). And that's why I don't mind writing the story about how I lost it with my daughter and the horse. I can boast in my weakness because Jesus is strong. I have nothing to prove because he has proved it all on my behalf.

The "good mom" law tells me there is no room for error; it says I must find within myself the strength to be perfect. There is even a "Christian good mom" law floating around in some circles which suggests that if I am unable to be perfect "even with" God's help, I must be an especially-awful person, or terribly immature in the faith. Sure, some believers struggle with one expression of sin, and some struggle with another. Some of us are more or less spiritually mature than others. But we all have one thing in common that the "mom laws" completely overlook: Christ met all the requirements of the law and poured out his grace upon each so we may be 100 percent acceptable before God…even when we fail.

Because I know God's immeasurable grace is extended to this sinful mom, I don't have to pretend all is lovely. I'm not afraid to share the ugly stuff because I know God's grace has already covered me. I am undeserving and defiled—absolutely, I admit it—yet he continues to pour out his forgiveness and draw me closer to him. And that is the infinitely more significant truth.

This means that although I hate my sin, I am also thankful for it. As my eyes have been opened to the wondrousness of God's grace, I no longer run *from* him when I blow it but *to* him. My sin is supremely offensive, but it also drives me closer to my Savior, and I am thankful for that.

Grace tells me I can royally mess things up and am still loved: this makes me long to obey Jesus. My desire is not to fly off into doing as I please, but rather to be near him, to walk hand-in-hand with the one who desires me, no matter what. I see this more and more in the way I deal with my family: when I sin, I come to God in repentance and find he has been loving me all along. How could I not desire the nearness of a God like that?

Grace Makes You a Lover of Grace

You may think I'm pushing this grace thing too far. Maybe you want to suggest some verses about not cussing or about loving my daughter.

Don't worry: I already know them. I even know the feeling—that burning to point out unrighteousness, or at least to shine a light on the better path—because that's where my heart goes as well. As difficult as it is at times to comprehend the grace God has gifted to me, it is even harder to stand back and let him give it to others. I'd much rather take matters into my own hands.

For instance, if someone in my family sins against another member in a big way, I want to solve the problem. I want to tell the people who have done the wrong how their actions were unacceptable and how it hurts others when they act that way. I want to list Bible verses that I think can motivate them to change, I want to make sure they know my disappointment, and I may even want to manipulate them into thinking God is disappointed. I want to tell them what to do, or tell them they need to make things up to the other person.

No, I don't just *want* to do these things—I often *do* them. I get all worked up about fixing the problem and neglect to love the people. It's what we do as sinful moms. We see sin and we want to zap it, thinking that if we really ream people out for the wrongs they do, then surely they will never do those wrongs again. Of course, it's fine and right to lovingly point out sin where others may not see it but need to address it, but think about how you usually go about that. Have you ever demanded someone else change? Do we have any right to do that? We are jealous of grace and want to call out the authorities to make sure everyone gets the public shame they deserve.

Remember from chapter three, however, that God does not love the way we do. There is nothing tainted about him; he can only love his children perfectly. He doesn't lecture us, nor does he withhold good things or send us away because he can't stand the sight of us. No, when we have failed to do what's right and have sinned against everyone within a mile's radius, our heavenly Father calls us over, lifts us up into his lap, gently corrects us, and lavishes us with his love. He tells us how much he loves us and how what we just did has been forgiven. We cry out to him as Father because *that is what he is* (Romans 8:14-17). Then he sends us on our way—not with a command of "be good and "try harder" or else I will be angry," but with tenderness, calling, "Remember who loves you! Remember the one to whom you belong!"

If you get this—I mean if you really understand that because of Jesus, God is not angry with you—you will not run toward sin like you might think, because when you know you are being pursued by a merciful Admirer, the lure of sin's crude pleasure loses its sparkle. This does not mean we will never sin, for as long as we are alive we will continue this present struggle against the flesh (Romans 7:17-19). What grace does, though, is make you long to be with the Father and walk in obedience—not because you are afraid but because you are loved. This means when you do sin, grace enables you to go boldly to God and even confess your sin to others where appropriate; grace makes you want to repent because you know you belong to the heavenly Father, and you want to draw nearer to him.

That's the irony of grace. If you are in Christ, you can do nothing to make God love you more than he already does. After all, he sent his Son to die for you! Neither can you do anything to make God love you any less than he does. If you take only one thing from this chapter, please remember that. Grace is a gift. Take it, live in it, delight in it!

Getting Real

1. Where do your thoughts go when you have really blown it like I did with my daughter and the horse? What verses can you give yourself in those moments of self-condemnation? Hint: see the first section of the Appendix.

2. After my scene with the horse, talking with a friend helped me start to see the situation in light of the gospel. There was a time in my life when this kind of helpful fellowship wouldn't have been possible for me because I didn't want anyone to know how weak I really was. Do you have anyone you can call in situations like that—someone who will help you see the gospel and see who you are in Christ when by yourself you can't even see straight? If not, is it because you are too afraid to share the ugly stuff or because you lack fellowship?

3. In the past, my temptation to punish myself to pay for my actions often overrode the truth of the gospel and showed my lack of understanding of God's grace. What do you run to when you have messed up? Do you punish yourself for what Jesus has already died for because you do not believe his sacrifice was enough? Or are you able to remember, repent, and rest because you know you are still loved?

4. How does remembering God's grace for sinners free you? How does this change your view of sin? Do you find yourself running *from* God in your sin or *to* him? Does your knowledge of grace make you want to sin more or walk in obedience? Why?
5. Do you truly believe you can do nothing to make God love you any more or any less than he does right at this moment? Why or why not?

Five
WEAK MOTHERING

We live in a world obsessed with strength. Parenting magazines feature fit, healthy, smart, confident moms on their covers. Our culture repeatedly sends the message that we must work hard to strengthen our physical, mental, and spiritual selves. If we are strong, we are in control, and strong moms are happy moms. Nothing can move the strong mom: she is a rock. In our world, strong is good, and weakness is…well, really weak.

I don't know about you, but I don't quite fit that mold. I am often physically weak, mentally exhausted, and spiritually wimpy. I find myself praying, "Lord help me—I can't do this" throughout my days. I thought this sense of inadequacy would begin to dissipate once my kids were all out of diapers, but it has only increased. Perhaps it's because they can all talk now, or maybe it's because I'm getting older, but I think it mostly has to do with my increased awareness of where I fall short as a mom.

Some days I am completely convinced I am just not worthy enough to tell my children about Jesus. I become ashamed of my failures and think the Lord cannot possibly use me in their lives. But in 2 Corinthians 12:9, God tells me just the opposite: "My grace is sufficient for you, for my power is made perfect in weakness." Motherhood has taught me how very weak I really am, and that is a hard, hard truth to accept. But by living in my weakness, I see more and more how powerful God really is. I come to understand that his power is shown to be perfect through my weakness and failures.

Living in My Weakness

If you were to read through my personal journal, you would see my main struggle is against my own weakness. Instead of boasting in my weakness so that the power of God may rest on me, I often find myself despairing because I am not strong like I think I need to be. I struggle with feelings of unworthiness as a wife, a mother, and a child of God—the proof of my unworthiness being my weakness. But through the power of the gospel, I eventually make my way to the truth, and the Lord draws me closer to himself.

You might be able to relate to this excerpt from my journal. As you read it, will you think about how you could also apply the gospel to your weakness?

Just when I think I might be able to do things right, there I am yelling at my family. Get them in the car and tell them how disappointed you are with them and watch everything "good" you've done fly out the only open window.

I tear them down, ruin their fun time. I am not worthy to be called their mother. I'm not worthy of this calling that is so much more than just feeding, cleaning, and clothing people. At times, it's as if I am purposefully hurting my family, relishing in my own glory of selfishness, giving in to all of the evil desires that have been manifesting in my heart. I want to make it up. I want to go and do something good to pay for what I've done, but Christ says, "No."

Christ tells me that I don't need to do that, and I don't like that. How am I supposed to feel better? How am I supposed to redeem myself and restore my reputation? Aha! There's the catch. I don't like grace. It's uncomfortable, and I don't want to take the gift. I want to throw it back and say, "This is not for me. I don't need your charity! I can do this myself!"

But can I really? Was I born of a virgin? Did I live the perfect life? Did I have the perfect ministry? Have I given myself to a death of torturous pain? Can I redeem myself?

I am not worthy of this calling. I'm not worthy to be named wife. I'm not good enough for those little faces to call me mommy. I can't justify or sanctify myself. I can't prove that I'm worthy because I am not. None of us are. I am just a simple-minded twit trying not to screw things up too badly. It is only Christ who is worthy in me.

My sin is beyond comprehension. I am nowhere close to good in my deeds. It does me no good to pretend I am strong.

My weakness precedes me. My weakness tears me down and leaves me as dust. I have no power to gather my own dust and put myself together. That takes an act of God.

It's when I am weak that I see his strength. I see how I am nothing but dust without him. I cannot produce goodness, kindness, gentleness, or anything else lovely. I am at the mercy of God's grace. The grace I want to refuse because I am too proud. The grace I want to refuse but cannot escape.

Grace grabs me and shakes sense into me. Grace envelopes me in his love. I am so ugly, yet he pursues me.

He won't let me go. His grace has me by the ankle when I try to run. It allows none of his children to escape, no matter how hard we try.

And then I give up the fight. I abandon trying to make sense of what I've just done. I stop trying to make it up to him. I give up trying to justify my sin. I no longer wallow in my unworthiness. Instead, I say "Thank you! Thank you for giving me your worthiness, Lord. Thank you for showing me once again that I have no righteousness of my own and everything I bring to the table is nothing but filthy rags." I can't make myself be a good mother—at least not for very long.

In this struggle of wanting to be better—to be something I think I should be and then failing to meet my own expectations—I so often forget that Jesus gave me his reputation. My worthiness is in him. He is my goodness.

And in all of this, while I rant and go on struggling with grace, the Lord remains still. He hasn't changed. His face is still turned toward me. He loves me as he loves his Son. He adores me and calls me righteous. He is dancing over me? What? That can't be! I've been too bad. But again he says, "No." He will never turn away no matter how many times I try to run.

"It is finished," he says. "Stop fretting. Stop trying to make this more than it is, dear child. Come to me and let me tell you how much I love you, and I really do. Be holy as I am holy."

He is so kind. He leads me to repent and soak in his grace. To marvel at what just happened, to run to my family for their forgiveness. Not needing to start over. Not needing to try it again until I get it right. Again he says "No more, my sweet child. Lay down your head on my chest. Rest and let me love you. This is why I did what I did; now believe it has been done. You are loved."

Living in His Strength

As long as we live in these bodies, we will continue to sin. Sin does not fully die in us until our bodies die; only then are we truly free of it. For now, we must accept that we will fail. So we must learn to live with the weakness of our flesh, but we must also understand that our deficiencies do not change who we are in Christ.

I hate not being able to do things right. I hate being weak. But in the infinite wisdom of God, he continues to show me that his glory is made perfect through my imperfection. Only in our frailty do we see our need for him. Only in his strength can we fearlessly admit our sin against God and others and seek true forgiveness. Only in our weakness does he draw near to lead us and use us.

When do you know that the Lord is near? The times I feel closest to him are when I mess up so terribly that I am on my face in repentance. That's when I fully understand his grace and his unconditional love for this weak sinner. That's when the second half of Romans 5:20 comes alive to me: "But where sin increased, grace increased all the more."

I don't always want to be a mother. Sometimes I try to persevere on my own, but that always leads to miserable failure, so I find myself in constant need of God's strength. A strong mother is not the glue that holds a family together; only a strong God can handle such a colossal task. My task, then, is not to conquer my inadequacy but to embrace it. If not for my weakness, I would not *need* God or forgiveness. I would not need to pray, I would not long to worship, and I would not desire the fellowship of others. In fact, I write these words out of my weakness. Weak is good.

In his commentary on Galatians 1:4, Martin Luther tells us that "Christ was given not for the holy, righteous, worthy, and those who were his friends, but for wicked sinners, for the unworthy, and for his enemies who deserved God's wrath and everlasting death."[2] That's you and me. If we were strong enough to conquer sin on our own, we would not need a Savior. Don't shy away from your weakness. Embrace it—and so embrace your Lord.

Only Weak Mothers Are Strong

Whenever my kids and I visit the feed store and peer into the warmers full of fuzzy days-old chicks, we try to find the strong ones. If it is time to add baby chicks to our flock of chickens, we pass up those with bald or bloody spots because the other chicks have bullied them; these are signs of weakness. We choose chicks that we think can survive the hands of four small children. We choose chicks that we can envision developing into strong, stout chickens that are good layers and, we hope, good mothers as well. Our selections disappoint us time and again as we find ourselves with unexpected roosters, hens that eat their own eggs, or hens that lay eggs with bad shells. But we always watch for the strong ones. Chicks showing the first sign of weakness are cast aside, deemed unworthy of our standards.

This is not so with the Lord. He does not seek the strong. Rather, he calls us out of our sin and weakness because Jesus is a friend to sinners. God loves our weakness and has never required us to have it all together, because he chose us *in the midst* of our weakness and sin. He saved us when we hated him and lived like the children of wrath that we were (Ephesians 2:1-9). He didn't look at us like chicks in a warmer and choose those who seemed to have the greatest merit or potential. No, he loved us and chose us despite knowing how weak we really are. Because God is omniscient, he knows every ugly thought, word, and action since the beginning of time. He knows all of my flaws, all of the times I fail to follow through. Yet he still chose me to be his daughter and give me everything that is his.

There is a danger here—being aware of your weakness as a mother can tempt you to wallow hopelessly in how terribly bad you are. After all, everything around us says weak is bad, even shameful. But the gospel tells us that when we are aware of our weakness, we must also remind ourselves of who we are in Christ and of the great power he has given us. Though the flesh is weak, the spirit is strong in those who have the gift of the Spirit residing in them.

I know this from experience because God has used me most effectively in others' lives when I go to my weakest place. When I fully unveil my sin to others, he flies in and speaks through me as only he can do, encouraging my children or my husband or a sister in Christ. It is not about showing them my holiness as a "strong mom" or demonstrating my worthiness so they will want to be just like me. Instead, it is about telling them what a great sinner I am and what a great Savior I have. There is no better way for me to live out the gospel than to be transparent about my weakness, especially with my family.

God uses our failures to prove—that is, to reveal the truth of—the gospel. After all, giving the gospel to others means proving that it was necessary for Christ to suffer and die (Acts 17:3). The gospel itself frees us to reveal our weaknesses to others and tell them where we find our strength. When by his grace we break through the shame and boldly unveil our weaknesses, grace rushes in and shows God's power to those around us.

Let me encourage you to take off the "strong mother" mask and embrace your weakness. Stop hiding the very inadequacy God wants to use to display the gospel. Believe his grace is sufficient. Allow his power to be made perfect in you and then boast! Boast all the more gladly so the power of Christ may rest upon you. In your weakness, you will be made strong.

Getting Real

1. How do you approach your own personal weaknesses? Do you use your guilt and despair to try to motivate yourself to "do better"? How does the gospel obliterate our need to be strong in the way that the world around us defines "strength"? What does the gospel say to mothers who fail?

2. Where does your heart go when you fail? Does it condemn you with the law? Or does it remind you of the gospel and God's unending grace for sinners?

3. Reread my journal entry and track my journey from sinning against my family, to despairing, to reminding myself who I am in Christ, and finally to praising God. How can this help you to see the gospel the next time you fail?

4. In what ways can we help other mothers see that God is glorified in our weakness?

Six

LIVING IN THE GOSPEL

If I've done a reasonably good job with this book so far, you may have arrived at this chapter with healthy anticipation. I hope you sense that because of Christ you really can start living out the gospel, and maybe you are looking forward to clear instruction on how to do that. Or maybe you've skipped ahead to this chapter in search of a handy checklist called something like "Six Steps to Finding Christ in the Chaos." (That's what I would have done.) But there is no checklist here. Sorry.

I'll admit, at first I intended this chapter to be about the practicality of the gospel—essentially a "list" approach. But after much prayer and thought, I concluded that in a sense the gospel really is not practical at all. That may upset you; frankly, it upsets me, because I want to know what to do! I want to change. I want to "get" it!

We all want to "get" it. We all want practical advice. *Just tell me how to fix my problem. Give me a set of procedures so I can complete my assignments and get on with my walk.* But here's the thing: God's first concern is our heart, our soul, and these don't respond well to checklists.

Imagine I really did have the nerve to offer you some kind of Godly Motherhood Checklist. How do you think any mom would likely respond if she actually tried to live by it? I know how I would respond. On days I followed the checklist closely I would exalt myself, and on days I didn't, I would despair. The list intended to promote my godliness would only tempt me to sin more. Now wouldn't that be helpful?

Instead, my desire is that God would use this book to *free* you to *rest* in Christ's outrageous grace, love, and mercy for you—*not* to motivate you to try harder.

Freedom from the stain of sin. *Rest* from our strivings to be worthy in ourselves. *Love* that never changes. *Mercy* for all our failures. *Grace* that saves eternally. These are things that Christ lived, died, and rose again in order to *give* us—precisely because we can't get them any other way. We can't achieve them and we can't earn them. No matter how strong or how good we are. No matter how hard we try. They are gifts and everyone knows a gift is to be received, not earned.

When our world, and perhaps even our local church, constantly tells us to try harder and do better, it is difficult to keep a sure hold on the message of the gospel. That message does not begin *or* end with our behavior or our performance. It begins *and* ends with the One who has fulfilled every good and perfect law on our behalf so that we may have hope in him. Is there work for us to do as Christians—as Christian mothers—because of the gospel? Of course. It is the work of remembering and believing, and then asking God to use us in our weakness.

All of us desperately want the key to a more abundant life. But we already have it. The key is Jesus. The key is not in somehow "being better," because being better is all about our invariably sin-tainted performance. "Being better" is all about me.

At this point in my walk, I think it comes down to this: We must trade in our performance obsession—which is really a sin obsession—for a Savior obsession.

Toward a Savior Obsession

When I hear myself talking with my family, and when I see the way I respond to them, I often wonder if I have ever even thought about the word *grace*. I wonder how I could possibly speak so highly of the gospel yet struggle so much in fleshing it out. Yes, I am completely unqualified in myself to talk about "gospel living." But the truth is, so is the next person. In writing a book like this, my only hope for maintaining any sense of personal integrity is to get over myself and understand that every single person around me also struggles to walk this out. The flesh is weak and fails us time and time again. The only one who could ever walk a perfectly gospel-centered life is the One who did so in order to rescue us.

Because of that, I live by hope—a confident expectation that God is continually changing me to be more like his Son. I know the further I press into the gospel, the more it will transform every part of my life. But the further I get down the sanctification road, the more clearly I see my sin. It can almost feel as if I'm going backwards, so I keep reminding myself of the promise "that he who began a good work in you will bring it to completion at the day of Jesus Christ" (Philippians 1:6).

There will never be a day here on earth when I can say, "By George, I've got it!" That's part of what makes heaven

so beautiful. Are you walking the Christian life because
you want to get to a place where you can think, *Finally!
No more chaos in my life. I'm so glad I learned to get all of
that under control?* If so, you are merely using the Bible
as a stepstool to glorify yourself. If so, you want the rules
of Christianity to help you become self-sufficient so that
you no longer need Christ.

Is that really what you want?

If I said, "Follow these steps to find Christ in your
chaos!" I would be saying there is a way to live beyond
the gospel. A place we can get to on our own that nullifies
our very need for Christ. But this is a book about living
in the gospel, not *beyond* it. The chaos of life drives us
to Christ and in this way he is glorified in the chaos. He
loves to show grace to sinners, dwelling with us when we
are scared and drawing us close when we have sinned. He
loves to show us his faithfulness amid the difficulty of our
lives. He loves to love us.

Because-Therefore

So far, I have tried to explain what it means to live in
Christ and enjoy his great grace and love for us. But I also
need to make a few points to help you better understand
how the gospel changes everyday living.

Some people say the teaching of grace encourages
Christians to become licentious and unconcerned with
obedience to Christ, or at least to adopt a flippant attitude
toward sin. My friends, this is not so! When we truly begin
to understand the immense scope of what Christ has done
for us, continues to do for us, and will do for us in the
future, we long to be with him. Until we really begin to
understand the gospel and its ramifications, we inevitably

see God as either an angry stepfather waiting for us to mess up or a heavenly Santa Claus who bestows goodies on us only when we've been nice. But when we understand that the God of grace has pursued us with a one-way love, we desire obedience. Our heart is crushed in our failures, not because we believe he will be angry but because we know how sweet the fellowship is when we do not wander.

We all know there are rich and glorious passages of Scripture which speak to how we should live, especially when life is hard. We realize there are commands directing us toward a way of life that honors the Lord and brings us greater peace. And we can all agree: it's not easy to live up to these commands. It's a daily challenge to put off the old self and put on the new, to love our neighbors as ourselves, and to submit to our husbands.

How is it these words of life inspired by the Holy Spirit can so often become to us a burden and a chore? Because we naturally tend to read the Bible simply as a manual for living, a kind of rule book. At that point, the commands of Scripture begin to look like a very large, very holy, and very scary checklist!

When that happens, we have forgotten that everything in Scripture points, not to our obligations, but to our Redeemer. We must always read the Bible's commands in the light of the gospel. Otherwise, what are often called the imperatives of Scripture quickly become just another set of obligations on our already out-of-control to-do list — when all along they are supposed to produce grateful acts of love for our Savior.

I have found it helpful to look at Scripture's commands in a "because-therefore" framework.

Because Christ died for you — making you fully

loved and fully acceptable before God—you *therefore* are able to obey the command to love your neighbor (for example) armed with a biblical understanding and a biblical motivation. This means you don't do good works to try to secure your position before God or man. You do it because your neighbor needs your good works, and because your good works serve your neighbor and give testimony to the goodness of God and your love for Christ.

You and I will never display love, joy, peace, patience, kindness, goodness, faithfulness, gentleness, or self-control in ways that are not self-exalting unless we do it out of a deep and abiding understanding of the gospel. If we do not live in the "because" (Christ's life, death, and resurrection) the "therefore" will become burdensome and we will throw in the towel when things get tough.

What the Gospel Does

Moms often ask me practical questions that boil down to this: "How does the gospel make any difference to me when I am in the middle of the real down-and-dirty, nitty-gritty stuff that happens throughout my day?" I ask the same questions, too.

What we do in the moment is not unimportant. But the gospel is not about *what* we do. It's about how deeply embedded Christ is in my heart. The gospel won't tell you what to do; it will remind you of what's been done by Christ.

This is why I say: as we apply the requirements of the New Testament to our lives, we must bring to this an obsession over our Savior, not over our sin. And this is what I mean when I say the gospel isn't practical. The gospel comes before the practical, and should inform how I handle the practical.

Now about that practical part…

When my 4-year-old is banging on his bedroom door as he awaits his discipline, or my 6-year-old won't stop crying and whining about my not buying her a turtle, or the school calls to say my son has just tried to run away, or my 11-year-old once again cracks open an egg under a hen to see if it's ready to hatch and kills the chick inside, or… how does the gospel affect me in the chaotic moment? Does it make me kinder? Sometimes, but not usually. Does it make me more patient? Probably, but I'm not especially aware of it.

What the gospel really does in my chaos is it tells me who I am. It forces me to get over myself, to be real, and to call on Christ for help because I understand more fully how weak and unloving I am. It frees me to desire what is right because I don't need to get my own way. I have nothing to prove because the gospel has reassured me I already have it all in Christ. Even when I forget that and stomp around the house trying to prove myself worthy of attention, Jesus is there. He knows I'm going to botch it up, but he loves me anyway. In those moments of chaos, the gospel frees me to believe I am still loved. It frees me to believe God is being glorified in that very moment — even in my sin — because that is what he does. The gospel frees me to believe there is no condemnation for me because I am in Christ and he will always glorify himself.

Do you believe God is as good as he says he is? When things start to unravel, do you first ask, "What have I done to cause this?" or instead do you ask, "What does the gospel have to do with this?" Living in the gospel means understanding that when things start to blow up, it is not because God is angry and paying you back. Rather, it means that, even as things are blowing up, you are aware God will redeem this current crazy moment for his glory. Living in the gospel means remembering the truth about who you are in Christ and why that matters.

The Gospel Goes Deep

The God of the gospel can carry you through even the toughest moments. Maybe not in the "victorious" way you have imagined. Sometimes you won't pull off more than a sloppy, floundering dismount. In any situation, the path you end up taking will rarely look like what you had imagined, but God will never leave you stranded and alone.

But know this: The mundane situations of real-life motherhood will always reveal how deeply the gospel has penetrated your heart. What you really believe about God will always be exposed.

One evening, my 4-year-old lost his "Bo," his beloved blanket. After searching for twenty minutes, I gave up and told him he had to sleep without it. Around midnight he woke me up crying for it, so I reluctantly began the search all over again, knowing I had already covered every inch of our small house three or four times. But as I began my search once more in the boys' room, I stepped in a puddle of wet carpet—clearly the work of someone with a larger bladder than our dog. My little fellow had stood up next to his bed, pulled his pants down, and just flat-out peed on the floor!

I began trying to explain to my son how irrational he had been. Half in a stupor, and wearing a sopping wet sock, I was getting irrational myself after a few sentences, so I changed gears. With much huffing and indignation I cleaned up the mess and continued searching the house for what I had now renamed "The Stupid Blanket."

It wasn't pretty. All I wanted was to crawl back into bed and go to sleep. Somehow I did find the blanket, but of course that's not the point of this story. In the midst of my grumbling, I started to give myself the usual, *How could you be such a mean mommy?* routine, but something stopped me and reminded me who I was. I remembered one simple truth: *I am loved. I don't have to act like this.*

What happened in my mind and heart in that moment was not complex or theologically tidy. Under the circumstances I didn't have the mental capacity to recall and rehearse all that Christ had done for me on the cross. But God knew my limitations at that moment, and he was good enough just to remind me, with fresh clarity, that even in that unlovely moment he loved me. I simply remembered Jesus, and this set me free from my guilt-induced anger so I could go love my little boy (who had since fallen asleep with his found blanket). Remembering how much I had been loved by God softened my heart.

My life does not always work this way. I don't usually have great gospel revelations in the middle of the night which cause me to love my family more. But it is always true that Jesus never leaves me where I am. His kindness always leads me to repentance, as Romans 2:4 says it's meant to do. His kindness is as much at work in me when I cry out to him amid temptation as it is when all seems to be going well.

The deeper the gospel goes in our hearts, the more we will start to see how it affects our actions. It is not about a formula or a list. If it were, the gospel wouldn't be the gospel. That's because the gospel is not something to *do* but something to *remember*. God has done for you what you could not do for yourself, and when you remember that truth in your chaos, you can live in grace. *That* is good news.

Getting Real

1. What did you expect from this book in terms of practical advice? Are you disappointed I have written no lists recommending how to live better in the chaos of life?

2. All mothers want to know how to improve as mothers. Do you find yourself disappointed when others do not tell you what to do and just give you Christ?

3. How can remembering how much God loves you help you in the midst of your chaos? Can you think of any personal experience in which you remembered the gospel and suddenly found yourself resting in Christ's help?

Seven
A NEW OBSESSION

One day my 3-year-old son called from the back seat: "Mom, did I grow yet?"

"You are growing all the time. You just can't see it," I replied.

"But Mom," he whined. "I want to grow!"

This conversation continued for the entire twenty-minute drive home. He kept asking me if he had grown yet, and I kept looking for an answer that would make him *stop* asking. When we arrived home, I unbuckled him from his car seat, lifted him out, and exclaimed, "Oh my! I think you've grown since we first got in the car." No, I couldn't actually see any change, but I knew there was truth in the statement. Besides, he was finally happy.

At age 3, my little boy was expressing the daily desire of my heart. With the same impatience, I ask the Lord, "Haven't I grown yet?" And just as I answered my son, the Lord assures me that I have indeed grown even though I can't always see it. But that's not an answer I like. I want to see big-time, obvious change right now!

Most of the time, I don't recognize I'm growing.

Instead, I often feel as if I'm shrinking. That's the funny thing about Christian growth. We have this idea that we should look and feel obviously more godly because, after all, God *is* changing us to be more like him. But usually, it's hard for me to identify any area where I have actually grown spiritually. And I think I know why that is.

I'm convinced that God keeps me from seeing my spiritual growth clearly because I would only want to take all the credit. That's how my heart works.

My son and I are both fixated on seeing change in ourselves. While my boy stretches to the sky, hangs upside down, and stands on his tippy-toes to try to become taller, I get busy making lists, trying harder, and guilting myself into finding the motivation to change. Though my son is indeed "taller" when he stands that way, he hasn't actually altered his height. So too, I can get busy "being good," but this never lasts long, because it wasn't real change to begin with; I was only pretending.

You and I might be able to contort our behavior into appearing more spiritually mature than we are, but we can't actually hold that position very long. Christ is the only one who can move us categorically and permanently from one level of spiritual maturity to another.

So how do we go about that business of change if we cannot produce the change ourselves? 1 Thessalonians 4:3a points us toward the answer, for "It is God's will that you should be sanctified." God wants to change us to be more like him, and he is doing just that. This is our starting point.

"Try Harder" Never Does Better

If you are like me, your walk of faith is not a constant stream of glorious obedience and you do not tend to your daily responsibilities crowned by a halo of grace and goodness. I have bad days, ugly weeks, and at times, entire months that leave me both wondering if God still loves me and marveling that my family hasn't voted me out of the house. I forget the beautiful truths I have tried to present in this book. I not only forget, but at times in my rebellion, I even reject them.

On days I am living in my disobedience and wallowing in my sin, I can convince myself the truths of the gospel are simply not for me. I can operate in the belief that gospel truths apply only to "good Christians" who are working harder than me. I will convince myself that my sin separates me from God, and that my lack of motivation to change angers him so much that he wants nothing to do with me because I am so unproductive in his kingdom. All great flaming lies from the pit of hell, of course, but sometimes it takes me a while to smell the smoke.

During these times, I think I'm never going to grow. I wonder why everyone else seems to have baskets over-flowing with the fruit of the spirit while my basket only boasts spoiled meat and moldy bread. So I start making a list of all of the ways I should change. I become obsessed with my sin but also with wanting to get better. I start working harder, only to fall into the predictable cycles of pride and despair.

I can be obsessive about my pursuit to get better. Honestly, I can easily consume an entire day trying to figure out how not to sin or, if that fails, how to patch things up with God. I know many of you are the same way. We are obsessed with pursuing *self*-sanctification. Tullian Tchividjian says the problem is simply that we think about ourselves way too much:

We spend too much time thinking about how we're doing, if we're growing, whether we're doing it right or not. We spend too much time pondering our failure and brooding over our spiritual successes. In short, we spend way too much time thinking about ourselves and what we need to do and far too little time thinking about Jesus and what he's already done.[3]

Only my Savior can halt that selfish spiritual downward spiral and bring me back to my senses. How? The Holy Spirit grabs my attention and takes me to Scripture. He tells me of God's grace and how I can never live outside of his love now that I belong to him (John 1:16; Romans 8:38-39). He reassures me I can do nothing to disappoint him, nor anything to earn his favor: Jesus has done it all for me (Ephesians 2:8-9). It is truly finished.

Why We Don't Need to Conquer Sin: A Look at Self-Righteous Self-Improvement

Over the course of several weeks while I wrote this chapter, I embarked on a quest to conquer my sin. I took my sin of impatience and anger with my children head-on, running hard to chase it down so I could slay it and rip out its heart to prove my identity as a "conqueror of sin." (I consistently neglected to remind myself that my identity is not "sin-conquering mom" but rather, "beloved, righteous daughter.")

I woke up every morning and told myself to "try harder" and "do better" so I would somehow be different than sinful old me. And I did become different—if acting like a bear to those around me counts. I constantly evaluated my performance as a mother and increasingly feared messing up. I became irritable and angry, resorting to tantrums and blowups directed at the very people whom I wanted to bless with goodness and kindness. I wanted so badly to change that I came to believe that people who were appearing to hold me back on my path to greater righteousness deserved to be taken out.

After one particular blowup with the kids, my sweet 6-year-old daughter wrote me a note to encourage me. Only instead of reading, "Dear Mom, You are the best" it read, "Dear Mom, You are the beast." She was only just learning to spell, so I figured it for a mistake, but oh how much truth that one letter had added! I had certainly been "The Beast" in my self-idolizing pursuit of holiness and Christian change.

As Christians, we obsess over being good and we can spend great effort on looking worthy of the Christian walk. That obsession can turn us into beasts. We tell each other that if we act, dress, school, and speak in a certain way, we will make Jesus look irresistible. We apparently don't want to believe that there are no "good Christians" and all our righteous deeds are like a polluted garment (Isaiah 64:6). In fact, it's not our goodness that makes Jesus look beautiful. It's his radical love for us *in* our badness that makes others want to know him more.

Do you want *more than anything else* to act better? If so, you will inevitably despair and question God: "I'm trying Lord! Why won't you allow me to succeed? What am I doing wrong?" We live as if we have never heard the promise in 1 Thessalonians 5:23-24: "Now may the God of peace himself sanctify you completely, and may your whole spirit and soul and body be kept blameless at the coming of our Lord Jesus Christ. He who calls you is faithful; he will surely do it."

So what is the remedy for this sin obsession and self-focus? Do we simply turn our attention toward others, trying harder to produce love and good deeds? Surely if we busy ourselves by serving others and conjuring up love, then we will be too consumed with acts of kindness to think much of ourselves…right? Not at all.

The attention we lavish on others can simply become a mask for self-focus, as we dive deeper into our "sacrificial mom" identity. When done by the strength of our own efforts, even good works only end up in self-glorification. Sure, exercising even a superficial kindness is better than snapping at my kids—this is an example of exercising the spiritual fruit of self-control, and that's a good thing that certainly does bring a measure of glory to God. But as with everything else in the Christian life, your motivations are what's paramount. If your good deeds result from mustering your will to "do better," they still come from a sinful heart.

Does that fact make you want to give up? Throw your hands in the air and declare that if your efforts are void then you will just live for yourself?

Don't despair so quickly, friend. Though focusing primarily on sin (whether your own or that of others) may be outside of God's will for you, your sanctification is not. He truly desires for you to change, but only *he* is big enough to do that job. When God wants to accomplish something, then it certainly will be done. And when he wants to accomplish something, he uses *his* power—not your strength, not my mustered will—to make it happen.

We must stop obsessing over our Christian growth and start obsessing over our Savior! Christ died in part to mature you in the faith. Don't you think he will do just that? In his time and in his way? Philippians 1:6 says, "And I am sure of this, that he who began a good work in you will bring it to completion at the day of Jesus Christ." So if you have known anything of the life-transforming power of God's grace, he is yet working in you. You may not see it clearly all the time, but that doesn't mean it's not happening. God has made a promise to bring you to completion, and he will. He tells us this because he wants us to rest in his work instead of working hard to make ourselves worthy.

God Doesn't Need Our Help

In this life, no Christian is ever perfectly godly or perfectly holy. But the flip side of this obvious truth is that, because we have the Holy Spirit living within us, every Christian possesses a measure of actual godliness and actual holiness. These came to us as gifts at the moment of our conversion. We didn't create them, we didn't give them to ourselves, and we didn't make them our own. They are from God.

Somehow, though, we often think becoming *more* godly and *more* holy is something we basically do all on our own. We act as if spiritual fruit is like choosing produce at the grocery store. Go to the right aisles, take bits of God's character off the shelves, put them in our cart, and scratch them off the list.

That's not how the Bible portrays spiritual growth. I'm not saying the secret to spiritual growth is passivity. We are called to obedience as a way of expressing our love for God and witnessing to others (2 John 1:6 and 2 Corinthians

9:13). We are called to serve others for the good of the body (Galatians 6:10). We are called to press on in the gospel (Philippians 3:12). But like I have said before, if we do these apart from a deep understanding of God's love for us they merely fuel our efforts to sanctify ourselves. We go wrong when we elevate in importance our puny, incomplete, and usually selfish efforts above the perfect, finished, and selfless accomplishments of Christ. We work hard and strive, but we go wrong the moment we begin to rely on our own goodness and strength actually to produce the change.

No clear and obvious change yet? That must mean I have to try harder!

Wrong. God calls us to live out our holiness, not by relying on our performance—trying harder and working feverishly to produce our own good works—but by *walking in the holiness we already possess through the Holy Spirit.*

To paraphrase Paul in Galatians 3:3, are we really so foolish that, having come to salvation entirely by the power of God, we imagine we are now being perfected by our own sin-tainted efforts? Apparently, the answer is "Yes, quite often we are that foolish."

The biblical way of change is this: We *do* what God has called us to do, even when it may not be easy, but we rely on God, leaving the specific outcomes to him, trusting he is bringing about the changes he wants in our lives and in the lives of those around us in his way, at his time, by his power and grace.

What spiritual growth actually comes down to, then, is getting used to the implications of your salvation, and this is a mysterious thing indeed. God has saved us and is now in the process of changing us because of "this mystery, which is Christ in you, the hope of glory" (Colossians 1:27). As you press on, remember who you are and that he saved you when you were yet his enemy: that alone produces change in the heart.

Wanting to love others, desiring to serve our family unselfishly, aspiring to have more patience with the kids — these are good things. I pray for these characteristics every day because they honor God. But if I am simply focused on getting "better" *rather than honoring God by living out the reality of the Holy Spirit living within me,* then all of my pursuit of "good things" becomes merely selfish. When we focus on ourselves in this way, we become ineffective and never actually change. It's like we're trying to accomplish the spiritual marathon of life with sprints of goodness, only to find ourselves exhausted and even defeated once the pride wears off. You can't run the long haul like that.

When we are obsessed with our own performance, we grow blind to the fact that we bring nothing to the business of Christian change. But that's the reality. That truth frustrates us and frees us all at the same time: as dedicated do-it-yourselfers we want to bring something into the mix, but that's not how God works. We want to help him out a little, thinking it might gain us some overtime pay — a little extra bonus of pride, if you will. Instead, God merely calls us to rest in him and walk with him as he desires to change us. What could be more liberating than to hear that a lifelong project that overwhelmed you, that you worked yourself to death on, is no longer your responsibility? That's freedom. That's what the Holy Spirit working in you means.

The Liberating Gospel Intervention

We have an obsession disorder, and the only thing that can bring us help is the gospel. In order to stop the madness of our self-absorbed efforts at self-sanctification, we must turn our sin obsession into a Savior obsession. And we can only do that by remembering the gospel.

The gospel tells us that Christ came and lived out the law perfectly on our behalf (see Romans 8:1-4). He did all of it exactly the way it needed to be done. He respected his parents when he could have usurped them by virtue of his heavenly authority. He was perfectly patient with his younger siblings' arguing when he could have silenced them with the snap of his fingers. He never spoke in an irritated tone of voice, never sighed with annoyance over someone's mistake, and never pretended not to hear someone in need. Jesus never needed to change.

Jesus did all of this for us because he knew how imperfect we are and how we could never make enough sacrifices to please his Father. He therefore offered his own flesh and blood as the ultimate and final payment for our reconciliation (Hebrews 10:10-14, 18). His blood was shed and *we* received the gift of his righteousness; he lost everything to give us life through his perfect, flawless surrender.

When I think about this—the shedding of blood, the forgiveness and righteousness given to me as an act of mercy—I can't help but run to him and ask him what he wants me to do next. I want to walk closer to him and hold his hand, ready to serve him however he asks. I want to show his love to others, passing on the grace I've been given. Change happens, but not because I get obsessed with self-improvement and muster up the strength to act holy; it happens because I am drawn near to my Savior.

When I obsess over what Jesus has done and marvel at his outpouring of grace toward me, I am moved out of myself into more Christ-likeness. That's when I am surprised into obedience and wooed into life-transforming change—not just a standing-on-my-tippy-toes kind of change but true, lasting life-change that happens from the inside out. Jesus desires that kind of change in me, so when I am afraid I'm not changing enough (or at all) and start making my "do better" list, I need only to run back to him and remember his promise to complete me. Philippians 1:6 tells me he *will* do it.

Christ alone will get us to the end. Christ alone is faithful to make us like him and prepare us for the final day. Rest in the peace of knowing his promise is good. Be free and get ready to enjoy the feast he has prepared for you. Delight in his never-ending grace. Take in a nice deep breath of the gospel and live in the holiness that is already yours through the Holy Spirit. He is worthy of your obsession.

Getting Real

1. Where does your desire to change come from? Are you are afraid God won't love you if you don't change? Do you believe he is changing you even when you can't see it?
2. What sins are you tempted to obsess over in your own life? What sins do you tend to obsess over in the lives of your children or husband?
3. In what areas of your life have you seen real, lasting growth? Remember the illustration about my son

and contemplate your "tippy-toe" efforts versus
God's work: where have you seen change because of
the Holy Spirit working in you?

Eight
TAKING OFF THE MASKS

One day when my kids were all under the age of 5, I sent a desperate email to a friend and mentor who has children older than mine. It said something like, "Please tell me I'm not going to ruin my kids!" Having already lost my temper several times that day, I had fallen into a pit of guilt and despair wondering if there was any hope for such a horrible sinner as me. I realize now my request was really a cry for the gospel. I had forgotten about God's sovereignty and I needed to hear about his unending grace for me, even on the really bad days.

My friend's reply was a guilt-inducing disaster. She basically said she couldn't promise I wouldn't ruin my kids, then she piled on some parenting tips and a few handy verses to help motivate me to do better. It was all we knew how to do in those days. So while honestly trying to help, she had only given this overwhelmed, guilt-stricken mom even more to do—a heavier burden when I could not even bear the first one.

Neither of us really understood the gospel. We were two theologically clueless Christian women trying our best to earn favor in the eyes of God and man by living up to a standard that we were quite sure was the only true definition of an excellent, godly mother. From my vantage point, I was failing miserably while she was soaring. She was a well-mannered wife and mother who loved her well-mannered children, and against that I just couldn't measure up.

Perhaps a better response from my friend would have included honest identification with my struggles. Something like this:

> I'm so sorry you are having a bad day. I had a really horrible day like that last week and yelled at one of the kids. I found it so hard to be patient with all the crying and just wanted to hide. I had the same thoughts you are having right now, but the Lord reminded me that I'm not the one who saves my children: only he can do that. Believe you are receiving his grace—right now at this very moment. Believe his love for you has not changed despite the fact that you have not loved your children well today. God's love is never based on our behavior. Look to Christ when you are tempted to yell, and remember he lives in you. He will help you through the most difficult times. Go to your little ones and ask them to forgive you. Tell them that Mommy is a sinner who has a great Savior. Pray with them and believe there is nothing you can do to thwart God's plan for them. We are all bad moms. That's why we need Jesus.

My friend's "do better" advice, although well-intentioned, amounted to more imprisonment when she could have offered me the freedom of the gospel. Do you see the difference? We must learn to give one another the freedom of the ever-good news.

Enough with the Masks!

As women, we love to look put together. We want people to appreciate us, but we just don't think others will find "the real me" acceptable. So we wear masks. We hide our weaknesses and hope no one will ever learn the truth. We get so good at it we might not even realize we're doing it. We give advice that we mean sincerely but that only imprisons others with mommy laws. We put our hope in the phrase "fake it until you make it" but wonder if we will ever actually make it and don't even know what "making it" looks like.

We've perfected the "I'm doing fine" smile for Sunday morning even when the world seems to be falling apart around us. We believe ripping off the mask might scare others away. We are convinced that if people see us crying on a friend's shoulder, they might think we have "issues." But we all have issues: the church is full of hurting people. Some just hide it better than others. That's why Steve Brown, in his wonderfully freeing book *A Scandalous Freedom*, encourages his readers to take off "The Mask of Acceptability:"

> When the requirement for acceptance in any particular group is to think certain thoughts, to act in certain ways, and to fit in certain molds — and we don't think or act that way or fit the mold — we tend to fake it. We put on a mask that says, "I'm just like you. Now, will you please love me and accept me?" I can think of

hardly anything that will kill your joy and freedom more than wearing a mask geared to get others to accept you because you are acting like them.

Allow me to let you in on a secret: *Nobody* fits the mold, and most of us wear masks to cause others to think we do. The greatest tragedy of the church is that, in many cases, the most dishonest hour of the week is the hour we spend in church.[4]

How can we break out of this pseudo-Christian culture that looks more like a masquerade ball of self-righteousness than an honest local church? How can we as women help free each other from the tyranny of "try harder" and "do better"?

Let's start by leaving our hiding place and sharing honestly with others. Let's boast about our weakness instead of putting on more layers to cover it up. When we hide our weaknesses and pretend we have everything figured out, we merely teach others (especially our own families) to be Pharisees.

This must stop! We must stop feeding each other the "try harder" and "do better" pep talks. We must start loving each other in our weaknesses, reminding one another of God's great grace for sinners—which includes each one of us.

Embracing Silence

Are you the kind of woman whom others could trust to really listen if they needed to confess something hard? Are you the kind of woman who could speak the gospel and offer ongoing encouragement to walk with someone else through hard times? Let's take down the masks and let God be glorified. Acknowledge your weakness, abide in Christ, and start breaking down the culture of self-righteousness. One way we can do that is by simply embracing silence.

We must stop talking and start listening, allowing the Holy Spirit to work through our conversations instead of giving each other advice that just adds more to the already crowded list of things to do. We are smothering each other with well-intended input when we often need to just listen and pray. There is a time and place to help others learn better skills for mothering and life, but when someone confesses a spiritual need, leave the "how to" behind and let the Holy Spirit lead.

We need more of, "I don't know exactly how you are feeling right now but I am here for you. Let's pray." And we need less of, "I know exactly how you feel. Try adding this to your diet or that to your schedule. That helped me." When we give each other more to do, the hurting mom is guilted into silence and walks away with a fresh list of handy self-improvement techniques that will either leave her discouraged or simply force her to pretend harder that everything is OK.

Not everything has a solution or an answer. It's alright not to know what to say. Take a lesson from those friends or older women who do not give answers so much as point others to Christ. The Proverbs tell us fools talk a lot, while the wise don't tend to say much (e.g., 15:28). This means the truly wise don't constantly trot out tips on how better to manage the chaos. They know how much our real need is simply for Christ.

Many times in conversation with other moms, I say too much. It's not always because I imagine I can solve their problems. Sometimes it's because I'm not really listening.

Other times I am so glad to be having an adult conversation that I thoughtlessly share whatever comes to mind. But I'm learning it's okay to say nothing. I'm learning to say, "I haven't experienced the pain you are feeling, but I do know it hurts, so I am praying for you and I love you. Let's have coffee." No Bible verses to motivate change, no advice given—just a listening ear and a reassurance of God's love.

A Culture of Honesty and Wisdom

An amazing thing happened when I started to apply the gospel to those areas of my life that I am always so tempted to fix on my own. By which I mean every area of my life. One by one, the façades I clung to so tightly started to drop away. I began to see how my pretending just hurt others and myself. The more I began to share about my brokenness, the more comfortable I was with it. For the first time, walls were falling down between me and other women. Women whom I had once deliberately pushed away with my parade of accomplishments began sharing with me like never before. My transparency became a key that unlocked a whole new level of friendship with others.

All I did was stop giving advice and start getting real with people. I started sharing my struggles as a needy, broken sinner thankful for God's grace. I started asking for prayer for more than my grandma's cousin's big toe. I let people in, and I let them see the ugly. How could I do that? Because the gospel proves I don't need any acceptance other than what I already have through Christ. When I embrace that, I am free to stop spending my time and energy trying to prove myself.

It's not that I'm now thoroughly transparent with

everyone. Honestly, I am still weak in this area. But my experience has helped me see how much a local church needs a culture of honesty, especially among women. We need wisdom as well—sharing your weaknesses and sins with others can certainly go too far—so let's use discernment. Save the serious stuff for your closest, most trusted friends. Let's also remember it is *our* sin we want to be transparent about—not that of our husbands, for example. We also don't want to gossip, and we must be careful what we say in front of children.

All that being said, God intends us to live in close relationship with others so we can have a safe place to confess our sin. And we will never get there if we aren't building relationships in which it is okay to discuss issues of abuse, the sin of pornography, thoughts of suicide, or other sensitive struggles that require tender love and wise counsel.

So don't tell your family secrets to the world just because you want to be real. But please do share your heart. Share your humiliating failures and ask for others to lift you up. Confess your sins of jealousy, pride, and hate to those around you. Let these things out into the light and be free. Then watch those around you become a little more free when they hear that you are just like them and that the gospel says God is glorified in just that kind of weakness. When our lives show our humanity, it gives to others the beautiful and much-needed permission to be human themselves.

Embracing Our Disfigurement

Well, we just talked about honesty, didn't we? Ok, then...

There was a time in my life when I relied heavily on masks. Lots and lots of masks. I worked hard at making the outside pretty because the inside was a bloody mess. I lived in deep depression, denied God, struggled with eating issues, frequently cut and burned myself to deal with the pain, had marital problems…on and on it went. All the while, my girls wore pretty matching dresses while I homeschooled and led a Bible study. Nobody had any idea that my life was crumbling to the point of nothingness. I was on the verge of ending my life, and I had built the walls around me so high that no one could see in and offer help.

The thought of exposing the real me seemed overwhelming. I imagined I wasn't brave enough to be honest with others, but my problem wasn't timidity. My inner screaming was muffled by sheer pride. Not until I had completely broken and the Lord began rebuilding me through the gospel did I see that God loves the broken and contrite heart (Psalm 51:17, Isaiah 57:15). Once I understood the depth of my failure and how I could no longer go on living the lies my masks portrayed, I was free to love a God who loves me even in my darkest hour.

My prayer is that those of you who can relate to the imprisonment I once felt would let down those walls before they come crashing down and hurt you. Allow the fellowship of the other imperfect sinners in the church, whom the Lord has provided for you, to infiltrate your life. If needed, seek out a biblical counselor to confide in. (If you don't know where to begin, try www.nanc.org/ Find-a-Counselor).

Maybe you have been living under your masks for far too long and don't feel you can survive without them. The masks have become who you are—not only to others but also to yourself. You may wonder who you will be once the real you is unveiled, and whether she will be anyone others can love or even care about. But honestly, we are all disfigured under our pretty masks. Once everyone starts to see who we really are, that's when the freedom comes.

When you live in the light of the gospel—you are set free from your incessant need for approval, whether from others or yourself. You begin to see the depths of your sin and unworthiness—a painful but necessary first step. Once you start to see that every effort you make even to serve others or obey God is tainted with sin, you will begin to see how much you have needed to be rescued by the only One who can make you worthy.

So do not despair when you see the real you. Your value is not based on the good things you do or how much you love yourself but rather on what Christ has done for you and how much you are loved by him. Working to please yourself or gain the approval of others is therefore pointless and irrelevant. Only one verdict of your worth matters, and God declared it on the cross long ago. Because of Christ's righteousness imparted to us on that day, we are esteemed as his beloved daughters with whom he is well pleased. All other verdicts have been tossed aside.

That means we really *can* be real and throw away the masks. We no longer need to hide our sin and imperfections because we know that God's approval is the only verdict that matters. We can agree with those who accuse us because we know the depths of our sin. We can rejoice in the great grace God has shown us because we know how little we deserve it.

Taking off the masks, being real, and living in freedom—this is a process. After all, it takes some time to get to know the real you. This is not about loving yourself more and embracing the "you" that you were always meant to be. No, this is about seeing the *real you* in the real Light. It is a good thing to feel horrified by the real you and run to the only One who can save you from yourself. The gospel frees you to believe that there is no "making it" and therefore you can stop "faking it." You already have everything you need through the righteousness earned for you on the cross.

If you believe these truths, the masks you wear will begin to melt away. Then, bit by bit, we can help one another become free as well. Allow other moms to be imperfect. Allow yourself to be imperfect. Be free!

Getting Real

1. What areas in your life do you not want to discuss with others? With what groups of people do you clam up or act a certain way to avoid revealing the real you? Why?

2. Why is it so hard to open up to others about the dirt in our lives? How does the gospel free us to do just that?

3. What do you think would happen in your relationships if you were more transparent about your sin? How could your transparency help your sisters?

4. Describe the interaction you see between women in your church, in Bible study groups, among friends, and in other gatherings? Are you open and vulnerable with one another or does everyone hide behind a mask? If the communication is not open, why do you think that is the case? In what ways can you help effect change?

Nine
THE COMPARISON CRUD

My kids are sinners and I have the video to prove it: four sweet children show off their masterfully crafted cupcakes to the camera until two of them begin to argue, then yell, then scream at each other before I finally turn off the camera in laughter and horror. Nothing but sin all around that day, words spewing out of my mouth that I regret to this moment. Desperation overcame me when I realized their sin was out of my control.

The Cupcake War, as I now call it, was just the beginning of a week full of arguments between two of my children. Every waking moment together they had a snide remark here or a push there, always culminating in a screaming match. They probably spent more time in their rooms that week than in both their lives combined; it seemed like the only way to keep them from killing each other. Did I discipline? You bet. Did we talk? Yes. Did I pray with them, point them to Jesus, tell them I loved them? Over and over again. But nothing seemed to help.

What conclusion did I draw after several days of

this mayhem? That I just wasn't good enough to mother them. Surely if had tried harder, handled things better, and generally operated more faithfully, then certainly my children would not sin this way. I acted as if the power to change my children's hearts belonged to me, and I blamed myself when they didn't budge.

By the end of that exhausting week, I felt crushed by my inability to be the kind of mother I thought I should be. At one point I even voiced to my children that a particular friend (we'll call her Carrie) was a much better mother. I felt ill-equipped for the difficult job of mothering and thought I could never match the excellence I thought I saw in Carrie and her family.

"She's the Better Mom, and I Hate Her for It"

Throughout that hard week, in my mind I compared my family to Carrie's. My children flung hateful words at each other—words I had never before heard come out of their little mouths. I was sure Carrie's children had never sinned this way. And I was also sure Carrie had never sinned the way I had. I began to think Carrie was more pleasing to God because of how sweet her kids always seemed. All I heard was how well-behaved her kids were. I became so despairing over my children's behavior and my inability to change their hearts that every time the fire in their eyes began to flare up, my eyes would fill with tears.

Weary after the weeklong battle, I dragged myself into church. Feeling burdened with my sin and dead to God's Word, I hoped for some encouragement. As I poured out my heart to a friend who loves me and my children, telling her how I couldn't believe the way my kids and I were behaving and that I'm sure Carrie and her kids had never acted that way, my friend stopped me in my tracks.

"Kimm, it sounds to me as if you hate Carrie." She said this in the most loving way one can express such a hard truth.

What? This conversation was supposed to be about pulling me and my kids out of this pit! I wanted to know how to apply the gospel to my situation. I wanted to know how to change my children. I did not want an entirely new problem handed to me!

But my friend was right, and as I slumped back in my chair, my heart sank. I had fallen into an ugly comparison war between myself and Carrie that was only feeding my anger toward my children and my hatred toward a dear friend whom I thought I loved. Every time I measured myself against Carrie, I fell short. And the further I fell, the more hostile I grew until my actions that week had become controlled by my desire to mother better than someone else — or at least as well. I now saw that the situation had revealed another problem, one much deeper than my children's disobedience or my abilities as a mother: I wasn't loving my friend!

My heart had drifted far from gospel truth. In my self-focused pursuit to prove myself worthy, I had forgotten about God's sovereignty and his perfect plan for our family: he gives us the exact children he wants us to have for our joy as well as our growth. He also gives our kids exactly the mothers they need; he uses our strengths *and* our weaknesses to help them grow. When I measure myself against God's law, I am indeed a bad mom, and my need drives me to depend fully on Christ as my hope and strength. As mothers, we can't ever be enough for our children. Only

Christ can meet their every need perfectly. Our hope as mothers should be in him and his redeeming work, not our own work. Praise the Lord for the fact that we can do that!

As always, God's kindness led me to repent of my actions and caused me to run to him, asking him to change my heart. When I stopped striving to be a perfect mom and began to abide in his goodness, I could focus again on the cross. And that's how God began to reveal to me what was fueling my self-comparisons to Carrie and every other mom I had known since forever. My Savior was opening the windows left and right, beginning to air out my stuffy heart and freeing me from the comparison crud.

"Stop It" Is Not the Answer

It would not be enough if I quit here. If I shared my story with you about how I had sinned, repented, and then moved on, the moral would seem to be, "Stop comparing yourself to others." But that wouldn't truly help anyone. For many of us, measuring ourselves against others has become second nature, like breathing. It's how we live, a way of marking out our existence: the comparison crud rules the way we dress, how we decorate our homes, and how we raise our kids. If you don't believe that, spend some time really thinking about what you do and how you do it and why. You probably struggle with comparison in at least one area of your life.

Let me go back and fill in some more about what I began to see in the midst of the Carrie episode.

As I thought about it, I realized that comparing myself to Carrie (and to others in general) was rooted in my desire for approval, and those roots ran *deep*. They still run deep. I don't want you to think I don't struggle with comparison anymore. That would be like saying I don't sin anymore. But I did have a genuine breakthrough. It was a breakthrough in understanding what the truth of the gospel means for my everyday life as a mom and a sinner. Because of that breakthrough, although I still find myself in the comparison crud from time to time, I don't have to stay there.

Today, I know I cannot measure up to God's standard, and that's why Christ died for me. I have seen this clearly in Scripture and God has stamped it on my heart by his Spirit. To really understand what my salvation means for daily life has been nothing short of life-changing. But here is an important distinction, an area where I can still trip up easily, and an area that horribly plagues so many moms.

Completely apart from my standing before God, I can find myself wanting to measure up to the elusive mom standard—not because I think God actually requires it but so before others I can appear to be worthy of this great calling of motherhood. Meeting God's standard through Christ is wonderful…but I can still desperately want to be admired, or at least not seen as falling short.

This is how the drift away from the gospel begins.

Isn't this true? We seek approval from friends, coworkers, husbands, children, pastors, grocery store clerks, librarians…you get the point. We also seek approval from ourselves. We want our performance to please others and satisfy ourselves. We work hard to keep up self-imposed standards because if we do, then and only then do we feel we have succeeded. We constantly look, evaluate, and change things to find the sweet spot that proves we are okay. Am I eating healthy enough? Am I diapering the best way? Am I spiritual enough? Did I save enough at the grocery store? Have I chosen the right exercise plan? Am I wearing the right jeans? And on it goes.

When this dynamic starts to take hold in my heart, to some extent it doesn't matter how solid my underlying theology is. Because if I don't push back against the craving for approval by reminding myself of my standing before God, then before too long my standing before God can begin to seem secondary. This, of course, is backwards, yet I start to live like it's true. I wonder if you do, too?

To put it another way, we can get so distracted by the horizontal (approval of ourselves or others' approval of us) that we quickly lose sight of the vertical (God's approval of us through Christ). Consciously or not, we expend great effort trying to please those around us. Think about your heart:

- How do you spend the bulk of your time? What motivates you to do the things you do? What motivates you to do them the way you do? Do you want to impress others?
- Consider the potential consequences if things changed or even caved in. What would actually happen if you didn't do the appearance-related things you can think are so important?
- Think about how you receive comments or observations. How do you handle criticism? How do you handle praise? Social media lovers: What happens in your heart when you don't get any "likes" on your Facebook status? Or how do you feel about yourself when someone retweets you?

When I look back on my day and see that I encouraged someone, received compliments, made people laugh, and appeared dependable and well-liked, I can easily conclude that people think well of me, at least in that snapshot of time. From there, while my head may not express it this way, my heart is breathing a sigh of relief—because God probably thinks well of me, too! How quickly can we flip truth on its head.

In the abstract I know God approves of me. But as I start to crave the approval of others it very quickly crosses a line, and suddenly I am seeing human approval of me as an affirmation of God's approval of me! The more I get hung up on the approval of others the more I imagine it to be a proxy of God's love. Soon, the settled fact of God's approval has faded and been replaced by this completely false yardstick.

And that means I am pretty much right back to the beginning, intent on proving my own worth to man and God. Almost as if I had never heard the gospel at all.

At that point, I simply have to repent and return to "living vertically." Sometimes I think I come to that realization on my own, and other times it is clear God has orchestrated situations which force me to remember. Either way, God works in my life to return me to the gospel I know to be true.

The beautiful thing is that the gospel speaks to each one of us right where we are, regardless of our circumstances. The gospel always works. The good news of Jesus Christ changes everything, flying in and obliterating my need to compare myself to others. When I live vertically, viewing myself only in terms of my relationship to God, I begin to see that I don't need to reach up to God through the things I do, nor do I need to gain his approval through others. He is already pleased! My heavenly Father showers down his grace and pleasure upon me because of Christ's sacrifice by which I was made righteous. Jesus lived a perfect life—a life fully approved by God—and his life is now and will always be my record!

Telling myself to "stop sinning" won't do any good if, deep in my heart, I still seek the approval of others and know that I don't match up to the standards I have for myself. Only the truth of the gospel—that I can live by faith in Jesus Christ because he loved me and gave himself for me—frees me from that comparison crud. So I return again to the cross and see my loving God dying for me. My eyes look up, and *then* I can recalibrate to see others on that horizontal axis clearly and quit comparing myself to them. I can love rather than hate because I know how much my God loves me.

Grace Makes You Free

Think about what Galatians 2:20 says: "I have been crucified with Christ. It is no longer I who live, but Christ who lives in me. And the life I now live in the flesh I live by faith in the Son of God, who loved me and gave himself for me." Doesn't that free you? What would your day be like if you truly believed this verse? If you really understood that it is no longer you who live but Christ who lives in you, that you are his beloved daughter with whom he is well-pleased—no matter what the people around you think, no matter whether your own heart condemns you. If you really believed it, wouldn't you experience so much more freedom?

God's grace is a one-way love—love and acceptance that flows down on us so we may in turn show it to others. A love we have done nothing to earn, grace as a gift. When we truly believe that this permanent, unchanging approval God has bestowed upon us because of Christ is enough, then we can receive compliments or complaints, approval or rejection, with a minimum of temptation to respond pridefully or defensively. Why? Because ultimately it's *not about us*. The good fruit in our lives comes to us from the grace of God. The bad fruit comes from a fallen world and the workings of sin, and because of the cross, our sins have been cast from us as far as the east is from the west. All that's left is the kindness and mercy of God. We can stop comparing ourselves to others because Romans 8:31 tells us that God is *for* us always and forever, whether we do everything right or not. Our identity is not in how others view us but in how God views us.

Romans 8 goes on to tell us: we don't need to find ways to fight our way into his presence. We are already there! Nobody can separate us from Christ who intercedes for us. When we receive the gift of his love for us, we respond in grateful obedience. We do not respond out of obligation (as though we must repay the gift). We respond out of gratitude and amazement over the fact that, even when we disappoint others or condemn ourselves, the face of God is still turned toward us.

Am I saying behavior doesn't matter? That we don't need to fight sin? Of course not. I'm talking about coming to an understanding of the gospel that will make you stronger in your battle against sin by freeing you from crippling guilt and pointless comparison. That's real freedom.

What would it be like to know this freedom? To say, "Yes, I'm a bad mom. That's why I need Jesus." Or "Yes, I've let you down again, that's why I need Jesus." Like Paul, we can learn to say, "I'm a wretched sinner! Praise

God for Jesus Christ my Lord" (Romans 7:24-25). What would it be like to put off false humility and really believe "no one can condemn me now because I am in Christ" (Romans 8:1)?

There is so much freedom in not having to prove yourself, in living according to God's plan rather than the expectations of others. Let's dig up that comparison crud—the sludge that has settled at the bottom of our hearts—and throw it out the window God has opened for us.

Being free of our incessant need to compare ourselves with others is not about telling ourselves we aren't that bad. Neither is it about assuring ourselves that our best efforts are good enough. It most certainly isn't about finding fault in others to relieve pressure from ourselves. These may pacify us for the moment, but we can find true and lasting freedom only in the gospel. God accepts his children without exception and loves them unendingly, not based on what they do but on what Christ has done for them. Christ has died to set you free!

Getting Real

1. List three mothers to whom you compare yourself.
2. How do you tend to make those comparisons? In what areas of your life and mothering? As you make these comparisons, do you tend to feel pride or despair? How does the gospel speak to pride and despair?
3. In what ways do you see yourself trying to gain the approval of God, others, or yourself?

Ten

REMEMBERING THE EXTRAORDINARY

I love watching a hawk glide effortlessly across the open sky. It's even more extraordinary to hear its whistling cry as it soars freely overhead. Every time I see or hear a hawk I remember the freedom I now have as a believer. That glide, that cry—to me these are little reminders from God of what he has done in my life.

When we first moved to the country in the summer of 2009, the noises of wildlife and barnyard surrounded us. I heard every rooster crow and every bird sing, and I am still trying to figure out the mystery animal we often hear after dark. Every morning of our first summer here, just as the sun would begin to filter through our bedroom window, I would hear the magnificent morning call of a hawk that had nested in a nearby eucalyptus tree. At first I rejoiced in nature's alarm clock that seemed tailored just for me. But as time wore on that hawk became an awful annoyance to me. I was tired of being woken up at the crack of dawn. Something extraordinary had now become ordinary, simply because I had lost sight of its significance.

Don't worry: I'm not going to tell you motherhood is like that hawk, something amazing that quickly becomes ordinary and annoying at times. I'm not going to remind you that your job as a mother is the most extraordinary and important job in the world. Frankly, that kind of talk scares the spit out of me. So I won't be exhorting you to go out and embrace your calling, love your family more, and be grateful for what you have. Of course, those are all very good things—go out and do them, but I don't think you need me to tell you that as I close this book.

Instead, what I want to do in closing is to remind you of how spectacular Christ is and how the gospel, though seemingly ordinary because we hear it so often, is in fact truly extraordinary. Like the sound of that hawk outside my bedroom window—had I reminded myself daily of how magnificent it is to wake up to something most people experience only rarely, I would have seen it as an extraordinary gift. It is the same with us: we need daily reminders of how extraordinary the gospel is.

Think about our Savior's humble descent to incarnation, his sinless life, his unthinkable death, and his miraculous resurrection. Remembering these extraordinary events will keep the gospel from becoming ordinary to you. We must repent daily of our unbelief that God really is as good as he says he is. We keep the gospel alive in our hearts when we regularly acknowledge our sin of thinking that the fate of our family rests on our shoulders rather than on his. We remember that the gospel is extraordinary when we run to the only One who can give us grace in our mothering. And what could be more extraordinary than recognizing our ability to rest in the finished work of Christ? God is glorified when we rest from our incessant desire to prove ourselves worthy of what he has called us to do. He wants mothers to rest in his strength and believe that he proclaimed the words, "It is finished," for you.

Remembering to Remember

During a particularly despairing time for me, my husband suggested I preach the gospel to myself daily to help me gain some perspective. I had no idea what this meant, and I'm not sure he did at the time either. I was not used to hearing "the gospel" used in any other way than to evangelize, and since I was already saved, I couldn't see why I'd need to hear something so elementary day after day.

I thought, *Okay, so I tell myself "Jesus was born, Jesus lived, Jesus died, and Jesus rose from the dead." Great, how does that have anything to do with the fact that I was up most of the night with a crying baby, the 2-year-old has had more accidents than I can count, the 4-year-old has been throwing screaming fits all day, and the 6-year-old is asking when we're going to do school? Not to mention that I haven't showered for three days, there is no food in the house, and I can't talk to my husband without crying!*

What I didn't understand was that Jesus' life, death, and resurrection had *everything* to do with my situation. The gospel is about the most thorough, selfless, and intimate act of love ever, and what my relentlessly hard circumstances needed more than anything else was the powerful and tender touch of true love. Not seeing this, I had failed to make the gospel personal in any sense beyond my initial salvation. I didn't understand that the gospel has daily power and application for me, personally. In light of my daily failures as a mom, I thought I could only address God from a distance. A clinging sense of guilt kept me believing that if I brought my failures into my relationship with God it would diminish his glory. I was convinced that, in order for God to look good, I needed to have my act completely together. I thought I could only really come to him cleaned up, in control of everything he had given me to do, and ready to serve. Surely God had no use for a broken mess of a mom who just turned her shirt inside out to hide spit-up. Surely God had no interest in a mom who had just eaten the blob of cereal stuck to her toddler's shirt because she was too exhausted to get up and throw it away. What could God do with someone like that? Why would he want to?

What I desperately needed was God's love. But I couldn't draw near to receive that love because I thought lousy mothers had no right to draw near. I didn't see that the gospel is just as essential to my daily walk with God as it had been to my salvation.

In his kindness, however, God perfectly orchestrated events in my life, counsel I received, and my desperate need to find hope in something other than myself, so I would find the freedom he desired for me. So I began searching out how to give myself the gospel every day, and I finally began to see how "preaching to myself" was in fact the most realistic and practical thing I could do. Martin Lloyd-Jones' book *Spiritual Depression* helped me understand this, because in it, Lloyd-Jones exhorts us to quit listening to ourselves and instead to talk to ourselves the way that David did in the Psalms:

Have you realized that most of your unhappiness in life is due to the fact that you are listening to yourself instead of talking to yourself? Take those thoughts that come to you the moment you wake up in the morning. You have not originated them, but they start talking to you, they bring back the problems of yesterday, etc. Somebody is talking. Who is talking to you? Your self is talking to you. Now [David's] treatment was this; instead of allowing this self to talk to him, he starts talking to himself. "Why art thou cast down, O my soul?" he asks. His soul had been depressing him, crushing him. So he stands up and says: "Self, listen for a moment, I will speak to you."[5]

Each of us are in a constant conversation in our heads. And because these ideas come from within and not from an outside source, when our discernment is more likely to be in gear, *we assume that whatever our minds tell us is true*. Many times, we don't even realize the lies we have been preaching to ourselves internally until we hear ourselves say them out loud. This is yet another reason why we need close fellowship with other believers who can help us discern the truth from the lies of our own heart.

Every week, each of us "hears" dozens or even 100 hours of this internal self-talk; your own heart and mind are your greatest influencers! We must learn to turn those hours of self-sermons into gospel encouragement, the kind we hear from the apostle Paul. We must become our own preachers of the true gospel, rather than the woe-is-me gospel of the harried mom.

Remembering to remember the gospel is not easy. Only through the purposeful re-training of our thoughts

can we speak to ourselves and bring comfort to our conflicted hearts. You can begin that re-training today. The
Appendix at the end of this book is divided into sections,
offering gospel truths for daily challenges that are
common to moms. Feel free to rip any of these reminders
out of this book and put them in your purse or tape them
somewhere you will see them often: the bathroom door,
the refrigerator, the car's dashboard or anywhere else
useful. Be intentional about rehearsing these extraordinary realities. Let the truth of the gospel comfort your
conflicted heart.

Repenting

Once you have done the hard work of remembering who
Christ is, what he has done, and the fact that he is in the
midst of and personally involved in everything happening
in your family, this will naturally lead you into repentance.
Not because of God's anger but because of his kindness,
just as Romans 2:4 states: "Or do you presume on the
riches of his kindness and forbearance and patience, not
knowing that God's kindness is meant to lead you to
repentance?"

Please don't read "repent" as meaning: *recognize
your sin, feel condemned, beg for forgiveness, feel unsure
that you are actually forgiven, and then "try harder"
to "do better" so you can get the guilt monkey off your
back*. Rather, read "repent" as meaning: *recognize your
sin, agree with God about your sin, and turn away from
it. Run to Jesus and thank him for his perfect life that you
cannot live. Thank him for showing you your unbelief.
Thank him for his grace for you. Ask him to change you,
and then accept freedom and love in your Savior."*

Keeping the gospel active in your heart requires continually turning away from your self-righteousness (thinking there is anything truly good or worthy in you apart from what Jesus has done for you) and self-reliance (thinking you don't need God's help at every moment in everything you do). Repent from believing that your worth before God is based on how well you are doing. Repent from caring so much about what others think of you, that it becomes more important to you than what God thinks of you. Repent from believing that your children's salvation depends on your performance as a mother.

Yes, God is to be revered and feared, and his Word is to be obeyed, but Christ died so we could actually draw near to him with total confidence that he won't squash us (Hebrews 10:21-22). Not only *can* we draw near to him as we are, with all the spit-up and cereal blobs and failure and despair—we *must*. Our union with Christ is intensely personal, and we can only experience and walk in the reality of that relationship if we bring to it the totality of who we genuinely are, warts and all.

So in all of your repentance, constantly remember who you are in Christ. You will sin. You will fail. Your hope, however, is not in your performance as a mother but in who you are in Christ. Take a moment right now to ask God to show you the areas of unbelief you struggle with as a mother. Ask him to forgive you and to remind you of where your worth is found.

Rest

First remember. Then repent. Finally, rest. Rest in the finished work of Christ for you.

As a mother, it never feels like I can say "It is finished"

about chores or caring for my children. But when Jesus said "It is finished" on the cross, he meant that for you and me as much as for any other believer. He was not merely declaring that his suffering had ended. He was declaring that the work of the law had been fully and perfectly completed on *our* behalf. His work was transferred to us as our work so we may be counted as perfectly and completely holy according to God's law.

In this, we can truly rest. We can rest in his finished work for us. We can rest in his ongoing work in us and our families, even when we don't see it. And we can rest in knowing that the weight of the world does not actually fall on a mother's shoulders.

Day after day, the priests under the Old Testament offered up sacrifices for the sins of the people. They could never sit down and rest because their work never ended; the world had fallen into a seemingly endless cycle of sin and sacrifice. But then God sent us the Great High Priest (Hebrews 10:11-14). Jesus is the only priest who could offer up a full and final sacrifice to atone for all of the sin of the world. He is the only priest whose work was ever finally finished. This is why he alone could "sit down" at the right hand of God: "So then the Lord Jesus, after he had spoken to them, was taken up into heaven and sat down at the right hand of God" (Mark 16:19).

Because of what Christ has done on our behalf, we can "draw near with a true heart in full assurance of faith" (Hebrews 10:22) and "sit down" in rest and completion. We can rest in the work he has done for us. We can stop the feverish work of trying to live up to self-imposed standards. We can stop trying to make ourselves worthy, because it is all finished. Believe it and rest!

The call to motherhood is not about you and your ability to raise your family; it's about a Savior who has called you to serve him as he fulfills a beautiful redemptive plan. Whether you are working joyfully or struggling to keep your head above water, he is loving you and working all things for his glory.

I hope that as you finish this book, you have a better understanding of God's love for you through the gospel, a greater sense of peace in the midst of your chaos, and a more complete sense of freedom in your heart. I certainly cannot manufacture those gifts and hand them to you with my words; only Christ can work in your life to bring you these things. My prayer is that he has done that very thing, or will soon, and that what you have learned will root ever deeper into your heart.

So I leave you with these words as one mom to another: run to Christ and seek his face. Tell him of your desire to see him in the midst of your chaos. And remember that when you fail to see him in your circumstances or don't desire to run to him…when you don't have the strength or the faith to keep the fire of the gospel burning in your heart, he is still there. His love for you never changes based on your actions. You are no less worthy of his love on the bad days, nor are you more worthy of his love on the good days. Because you are clothed in Christ's righteousness, your heavenly Father is delighted to have you as his child. He sings over you, loves you, and rejoices in you because you are his beloved daughter with whom he is well pleased. Go now and be free!

Getting Real

1. Has reading this book changed your understanding of the gospel? In what ways?
2. In what practical ways can you remind yourself of the gospel every day?
3. Has your view of God's love and grace affected the way you view motherhood? In what ways has the gospel freed you as a mother?
4. Describe in your own words what it means to remember, repent, and rest. How can these three Rs help you see Christ in your chaos?

Appendix—Gospel Truths

For When You Blow It

What do you do when you blow it? These gospel truths help me to get back to the right thinking when all I want to do is wallow in my sin.

His kindness leads me to repentance: "Or do you presume on the riches of his kindness and forbearance and patience, not knowing that God's kindness is meant to lead you to repentance?" (Romans 2:4).

He is not angry with me: "Since, therefore, we have now been justified by his blood, much more shall we be saved by him from the wrath of God" (Romans 5:9).

He saved me when I was his enemy: "For if while we were enemies we were reconciled to God by the death of his Son, much more, now that we are reconciled, shall we be saved by his life" (Romans 5:10).

Where sin abounds, grace abounds all the more: "Now the law came in to increase the trespass, but where sin increased, grace abounded all the more" (Romans 5:20).

Sin is no longer my master: "For sin will have no dominion over you, since you are not under law but under grace" (Romans 6:14).

Nothing I do can separate me from his love: "For I am sure that neither death nor life, nor angels nor rulers, nor things present nor things to come, nor powers, nor height nor depth, nor anything else in all creation, will be able to separate us from the love of God in Christ Jesus our Lord" (Romans 8:38-39).

My sin has already been forgiven and nailed to the cross: "And you, who were dead in your trespasses and the uncircumcision of your flesh, God made alive together with him, having forgiven us all our trespasses, by canceling the record of debt that stood against us with its legal demands. This he set aside, nailing it to the cross" (Colossians 2:13-14).

God is greater than my heart: "By this we shall know that we are of the truth and reassure our heart before him; for whenever our heart condemns us, God is greater than our heart, and he knows everything" (1 John 3:19-20).

There is no more judgment against me: "There is therefore now no condemnation for those who are in Christ Jesus" (Romans 8:1).

For When You Feel Weak

This world teaches us to cover up our weaknesses and only present the best of the best. Where strength is coveted, we become ashamed of our faults. Only the gospel frees us to admit weaknesses. Because Christ has lived perfectly for us, we have nothing left to prove and nothing left to hide.

When I feel weak, here are a few verses that remind me how the gospel speaks to my weakness.

It's okay to be weak! We can be content in our weakness because that is where God's strength is found: "For the sake of Christ, then, I am content with weaknesses, insults, hardships, persecutions, and calamities. For when I am weak, then I am strong" (2 Corinthians 12:10).

His grace is *always* sufficient and will always be poured out on you in your weakness: "But he said to me, "My grace is sufficient for you, for my power is made perfect in weakness." Therefore I will boast all the more gladly of my weaknesses, so that the power of Christ may rest upon me" (2 Corinthians 12:9).

The Holy Spirit helps us in our weakness:
"Likewise the Spirit helps us in our weakness. For we do
not know what to pray for as we ought, but the Spirit
himself intercedes for us with groanings too deep for
words" (Romans 8:26).

He understands our weakness: "For we do not have
a high priest who is unable to sympathize with our weaknesses, but one who in every respect has been tempted as
we are, yet without sin" (Hebrews 4:15).

**He first loved us in our weakness, so we don't have
to prove we are strong to earn his love:** "For while
we were still weak, at the right time Christ died for the
ungodly. For one will scarcely die for a righteous person—
though perhaps for a good person one would dare even to
die" (Romans 5:6-7).

**It is not until we see our weakness that we will
praise his strength:** "I was pushed hard, so that I was
falling, but the Lord helped me. The Lord is my strength
and my song; he has become my salvation. Glad songs of
salvation are in the tents of the righteous: 'The right hand
of the Lord does valiantly'" (Psalm 118:13-15).

Our strength fails but his strength goes on forever:
"My flesh and my heart may fail, but God is the strength of
my heart and my portion forever" (Psalm 73:26).

For When You Are Discouraged

Being a mother can be discouraging. The good we plan
for our kids seems to meet resistance more often than not.
What can a mom do when she feels she can't go on another
minute? Trying harder isn't the answer. Remembering the
love and grace the Father continually pours out on us is.
Here are verses to encourage your heart during those times.

Wait on the Lord and he will strengthen your heart: "I would have lost heart, unless I had believed that I would see the goodness of the Lord In the land of the living. Wait on the Lord; Be of good courage, And He shall strengthen your heart; Wait, I say, on the Lord!" (Psalm 27:13-14 NKJV).

Wait for the Lord expectantly: "Out of the depths I cry to you, O LORD! O Lord, hear my voice! Let your ears be attentive to the voice of my pleas for mercy! If you, O LORD, should mark iniquities, O Lord, who could stand? But with you there is forgiveness, that you may be feared. I wait for the LORD, my soul waits, and in his word I hope; my soul waits for the Lord more than watchmen for the morning, more than watchmen for the morning. O Israel, hope in the LORD! For with the LORD there is steadfast love, and with him is plentiful redemption. And he will redeem Israel from all his iniquities" (Psalm 130).

He bottles up every tear: "You have kept count of my tossings; put my tears in your bottle. Are they not in your book?" (Psalm 56:8).

His strength is mine: "My flesh and my heart may fail, but God is the strength of my heart and my portion forever" (Psalm 73:26).

He loves the brokenhearted: "The LORD is near to the brokenhearted and saves the crushed in spirit" (Psalm 34:18).

He will not burden the discouraged heart: "A bruised reed he will not break, and a faintly burning wick he will not quench; he will faithfully bring forth justice" (Isaiah 42:3).

He is never discouraged even when we are: "He will not grow faint or be discouraged till he has established justice in the earth; and the coastlands wait for his law" (Isaiah 42:4).

Even when we are discouraged and our faith is weak,
he remains faithful to us: "if we are faithless, he remains
faithful—for he cannot deny himself" (2 Timothy 2:13).

For When You Are Overwhelmed

Some moments of motherhood threaten to overwhelm
us. We often feel as if there is too much too do on too
little sleep with too few resources, and we wonder if we
will survive. What does a mom do when she feels overwhelmed? Take a deep breath of the gospel and find rest
for your heart in these verses.

God was *for* me before I could even speak his name,
and he remains *for* me today: "What then shall we say
to these things? If God is for us, who can be against us?
He who did not spare his own Son but gave him up for
us all, how will he not also with him graciously give us all
things?" (Romans 8:31-32).

"It is finished" means I can rest in the finished
work of Christ. There is nothing left to do that has not
already been done: "For we who have believed enter that
rest, as he has said, "As I swore in my wrath, 'They shall
not enter my rest,'" although his works were finished
from the foundation of the world" (Hebrews 4:3).

If God's grace was sufficient to fulfill the law
through Christ, then God's grace is sufficient for me
today: "For from his fullness we have all received, grace
upon grace. For the law was given through Moses; grace
and truth came through Jesus Christ" (John 1:16-17).

He will enable you to do what he has called you to:
"He who calls you is faithful; he will surely do it" (1 Thessalonians 5:24).

He promises that he provides never-ending love and mercy each day: "The steadfast love of the Lord never ceases; his mercies never come to an end; they are new every morning; great is your faithfulness" (Lamentations 3:22-23).

He holds everything together even when I cannot: "And he is before all things, and in him all things hold together" (Colossians 1:17).

He promises to walk with us in trials and not let us get overwhelmed: "When you pass through the waters, I will be with you; and through the rivers, they shall not overwhelm you; when you walk through fire you shall not be burned, and the flame shall not consume you" (Isaiah 43:2).

He is gentle with mothers: "He will tend his flock like a shepherd; he will gather the lambs in his arms; he will carry them in his bosom, and gently lead those that are with young" (Isaiah 40:11).

Endnotes

1. Elyse Fitzpatrick, *Because He Loves Me* (Crossway, 2008), 41
2. Martin Luther, *Galatians* (Crossway, 1998) 40
3. Ed Stetzer, "Jesus + Nothing = Everything: An Interview with Tullian Tchividjian , Pt. 3," November 9, 2011, http://www.edstetzer.com/2011/11/jesusnothingeverything-pt-3.html
4. Steve Brown, *A Scandalous Freedom* (Howard 2004), 108
5. D. Martyn Lloyd-Jones, *Spiritual Depression* (Eerdmans, 1965) 20–21

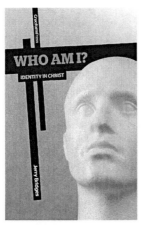

Who Am I?
Identity in Christ

by Jerry Bridges

Jerry Bridges unpacks Scripture to give the Christian eight clear, simple, interlocking answers to one of the most essential questions of life.

"Jerry Bridges' gift for simple but deep spiritual communication is fully displayed in this warm-hearted, biblical spelling out of the Christian's true identity in Christ."

> *J. I. Packer, Theological Editor,* **ESV Study Bible;** *author,*
> **Knowing God, A Quest for Godliness, Concise Theology**

"I know of no one better prepared than Jerry Bridges to write *Who Am I?* He is a man who knows who he is in Christ and he helps us to see succinctly and clearly who we are to be. Thank you for another gift to the Church of your wisdom and insight in this book."

> *R.C. Sproul, founder, chairman, president, Ligonier Ministries;*
> *executive editor,* **Tabletalk** *magazine; general editor,* **The**
> **Reformation Study Bible**

"*Who Am I?* answers one of the most pressing questions of our time in clear gospel categories straight from the Bible. This little book is a great resource to ground new believers and remind all of us of what God has made us through faith in Jesus. Thank the Lord for Jerry Bridges, who continues to provide the warm, clear, and biblically balanced teaching that has made him so beloved to this generation of Christians."

> *Richard D. Phillips, Senior Minister, Second Presbyterian*
> *Church, Greenville, SC*

The Organized Heart
A Woman's Guide to Conquering Chaos

by Staci Eastin

**Disorganized?
You don't need more rules, the
latest technique, or a new gadget.**

**This book will show you a different,
better way. A way grounded in the
grace of God.**

"Staci Eastin packs a gracious punch, full of insights about our
disorganized hearts and lives, immediately followed by the balm of
gospel-shaped hopes. This book is ideal for accountability partners
and small groups."

> *Carolyn McCulley, blogger, filmmaker, author of* Radical Wom-
> anhood *and* Did I Kiss Marriage Goodbye?

"Unless we understand the spiritual dimension of productivity, our
techniques will ultimately backfire. Find that dimension here. Encouraging and uplifting rather than guilt-driven, this book can help
women who want to be more organized but know that adding a new
method is not enough."

> *Matt Perman, Director of Strategy at Desiring God, blogger,
> author of the forthcoming book,* What's Best Next: How the
> Gospel Transforms the Way You Get Things Done

"Organizing a home can be an insurmountable challenge for a woman. The Organized Heart makes a unique connection between idols
of the heart and the ability to run a well-managed home. This is not
a how-to. Eastin looks at sin as the root problem of disorganization.
She offers a fresh new approach and one I recommend, especially to
those of us who have tried all the other self-help models and failed."

> *Aileen Challies, mom of three, and wife of blogger, author, and
> pastor Tim Challies*

JOY!
A Bible Study on Philippians for Women

by Keri Folmar

One of the few truly inductive Bible studies intended for use by women.

"This study points the way into the biblical text, offering a clear and effective guide in studying Paul's letter to the Philippian church. Keri Folmar encourages her readers first and foremost to listen well to God's inspired Word."

> **Kathleen Nielson, author of the Living Word Bible Studies; Director of Women's Initiatives, The Gospel Coalition**

"Keri's Bible study will not only bring the truths of Philippians to bear upon your life, but will also train you up for better, more effective study of any book of the Bible with her consistent use of the three questions needed in all good Bible study: Observation, Interpretation, and Application."

> **Connie Dever, author of The Praise Factory children's ministry curriculum and wife of Pastor Mark Dever, President of 9 Marks Ministries**

""Keri lets the Scriptures do the talking! No cleverly invented stories, ancillary anecdotes, or emotional manipulation here. Keri takes us deeper into the text, deeper into the heart of Paul, deeper into the mind of Christ, and deeper into our own hearts as we pursue Christ for joy in all things. I highly commend this study for your pursuit of joy."

> **Kristie Anyabwile is a graduate of NC State University and wife of Thabiti, a Gospel Coalition Council Member**

Friends and Lovers
Cultivating Companionship and Intimacy in Marriage

by Joel R. Beeke

Marriage is for God's glory and our good.

The secret?

Intimate Christian companionship.

"A book about love, marriage, and sex from Joel Beeke that is surprisingly candid yet without a trace of smuttiness. Fresh and refreshingly straightforward, this is the best book of its kind."
Derek W H Thomas, Visiting Professor, Reformed Theo. Sem.

"Marriage is hard work. And wonderful. And sometimes, it's both at the same time. *Friends and Lovers* is like a personal mentoring session on marriage with a man whose heart is devoted to seeing Christ honored in how we love each other as husbands and wives. It's full of practical wisdom and grace. A delight."
Bob Lepine, Co-Host, FamilyLife Today

"By laying the theological, emotional, social, and spiritual foundations of marriage before heading to the bedroom, Joel Beeke provides a healthy corrective to the excessive and obsessive sex-focus of our generation and even of some pastors. But, thankfully, he also goes on to provide wise, practical, down-to-earth direction for couples wanting to discover or recover physical intimacy that will both satisfy themselves and honor God."
Dr. David Murray, Professor, Puritan Reformed Theo. Sem.

"There is no better book than this to renew the affection of happy marriage."
Geoffrey Thomas, Pastor, Alfred Place Baptist Church, Wales

Intentional Parenting
Family Discipleship by Design

by Tad Thompson

**The Big Picture and a Simple Plan —
That's What You Need to Do Family
Discipleship Well**

*This book will allow you to take all the
sermons, teachings, and exhortations
you have received on the topic of
family discipleship, make sense of it,*

"As parents, we know God has given us the responsibility to train our
children in his ways. But many parents don't know where or how to
start. Tad has done us all a favor by identifying seven key categories
of biblical teaching we can utilize in teaching our children godly
truth and principles. This easy-to-follow plan will help any parent
put the truth of God's Word into their children's hearts."
> **Kevin Ezell, President, North American Mission Board,
> Southern Baptist Convention; father of six**

"Here is a practical page-turner that encourages fathers to engage the
hearts of their families with truth and grace. In an age when truth is
either ignored or despised, it is refreshing to see a book written for
ordinary fathers who want their families to be sanctified by the truth.
Thompson writes with a grace which reminds us that parenting
flows from the sweet mercies of Christ."
> **Joel Beeke, President, Puritan Reformed Theological
> Seminary**

"Need an introductory text to the topic of discipling children? Here is
a clear, simple book on family discipleship, centered on the gospel
rather than human successes or external behaviors."
> **James M. Hamilton, Associate Professor of Biblical
> Theology, The Southern Baptist Theological Seminary**

Brass Heavens
Reasons for Unanswered Prayer
by Paul Tautges

Does it ever seem like God is not listening?

Scripture offers six clear reasons why your prayers may go unanswered.

Learn what they are and what you can do about it.

"Paul Tautges scatters the darkness of doubt. He blends biblical teaching with practical illustrations to challenge and comfort us when the heavens seem as brass. Read this to revive your prayers, to melt the heavens, and to increase your answers."
David Murray, Puritan Reformed Theological Seminary

"Some things in the Scriptures are conveniently ignored...but this book will not let us continue to bury Scripture's clear teaching, or continue to ignore the ongoing rebellions, unrelinquished resentments, and unconfessed sins in our lives that may be hindering our prayers."
Nancy Guthrie, author, Seeing Jesus in the Old Testament

"Both motivating and convicting....Read and obey for the sake of your future, your family, and the work of God in the world."
Jim Elliff, President, Christian Communicators Worldwide

"Like the Scriptures, Paul Tautges does not leave us in the pit of despair, but shows that where sin abounds, grace superabounds—there are biblical pathways for dealing with our role in unanswered prayers and for responding humbly to God's affectionate sovereignty."
Bob Kellemen, Executive Dir., Biblical Counseling Coalition

Modest

Men and Women Clothed in the Gospel

by R W Glenn, Tim Challies

Modesty is about freedom, not rules.

What you say or do or wear is not really the point. The point is your heart.

True modesty flows from a solid grasp of the gospel.

"It is so refreshing to have a book on modesty that is a useful resource and not a legalistic, culture-bound list that leaves you a bit paranoid and guilty. No, this book is different. Its counsel on modesty is not rooted in rules, but in the grace of the gospel of Jesus Christ. That grace alone is able to get at the heart of the problem of modesty, which *is* the heart. In a culture where immodesty is the accepted norm, Glenn and Challies have given us help that every Christian desperately needs."
Paul Tripp, pastor, conference speaker, and author

"How short is too short? How tight is too tight? Glenn and Challies don't say. But they do provide a thoughtful framework to help us come to a grace-based, gospel-grounded understanding of modesty that extends beyond mere clothing. They uphold a vision for modesty that's both beautiful and desirable – and not only for gals, but for guys too! This book is a great tool to help you wrestle with the practical question of what and what not to wear."
Mary A. Kassian, Author, **Girls Gone Wise**

"The authors of Modest break new ground in their treatment of this difficult subject. It is a healthy antidote to the prevailing views, which tend toward either legalism or antinomianism, by grounding the whole subject in the gospel. I heartily recommend this book."
Jerry Bridges, Author, **The Pursuit of Holiness**

Wrestling with an Angel
A Story of Love, Disability and the Lessons of Grace

by Greg Lucas

The riveting, inspiring true story that readers have called "a touchstone book of my life," and "alternately hilarious and heartbreaking," a book that "turns the diamond of grace in such a way that you see facets you never really noticed before."

"C.S. Lewis wrote that he paradoxically loved *The Lord of the Rings* because it 'broke his heart'—and Greg Lucas' writing does the same for me."

Justin Taylor, Managing Editor, ESV Study Bible

"Witty... stunning... striking... humorous and heartfelt. *Wrestling with an Angel* provides a fresh, honest look at one father's struggle to embrace God in the midst of his son's disability. Can sheer laughter and weeping gracefully coexist in a world of so much affliction? Greg knows all about it. I highly recommend this wonderfully personal book!"

Joni Eareckson Tada, Joni and Friends International

"You will laugh; you will cry. You will feel sick; you will feel inspired. You will be repulsed by the ugliness of sin; you will be overwhelmed by the love of God. Greg Lucas takes us on an unforgettable ride as he extracts the most beautiful insights into grace from the most painful experiences of life."

David P. Murray, Puritan Reformed Theological Seminary

"Greg Lucas is a captivating storyteller. When he writes about life with Jake, I recognize God's grace and loving persistence in my life. I want more!"

Noël Piper, author, and wife of pastor and author John Piper